LOW FIRE

Other Ways to Work in Clay

LOW FIRE

Other Ways to Work in Clay

Leon I. Nigrosh

Drawings by Donald Krueger

Davis Publications, Inc./Worcester, Massachusetts

Cover Credits

Top, from left: *Pot of Gold,* 1970, author. High fired stoneware, glaze, luster, acrylic paint, thrown, slab built; Pot, 1979, Paul Soldner. Porcelain, slip, thrown, altered, unglazed, salt bisque fired; *Symbiosis, Schmimbiosis,* 1978, Bill Suworoff. White clay, underglaze, glaze, molded, hand built. Bottom, from left: *Raku Vase,* David Roth. White raku clay, glaze, thrown; *Indirect Object,* Eric L. Blecher. Talc clay, photo decal, glaze, slab built. Back cover: Bowl, David Joy. Bisque fired porcelain, thrown, altered, vapor glazed.

Printed in the United States of America
Library of Congress Catalog Card Number: 79-56377
ISBN: 0-87192-120-0

10 9 8 7 6 5 4 3 2 1

Contents

Preface

Working with low temperature ceramic materials takes on added meaning when one realizes that several generations of young potters have neglected creating objects at this end of the heat range. For more than twenty-five years attention has focused almost exclusively on high fire reduction stoneware and porcelain. The opinion that any form of clay fabrication must be fired high to be worthy of professional consideration is erroneous.

Leon Nigrosh shows that the whole range from low to high temperatures, not one or the other, can be used effectively, creatively, and should be investigated for fuller aesthetic development.

Working exclusively at top temperatures results in a narrowing of the color palette. Muted, earthy colors are produced by the interaction of intense heat and a lack of oxygen in the ware chamber during firing. These subtle colors are not undesirable except when ceramic objects appear to be of the same color tone all across the country. Such "natural" coloration of clay, bodies, and glazes gives an impression that only ivory, tan, brown, and black are available for surface enrichment. Ceramic ware in the marketplace and in exhibitions tends to be less interesting, less dynamic, when numerous objects have a close similarity in material, structure, and surfacing.

Change is underway, providing more variety and an intensification in ceramic color relationships. Leon Nigrosh is well qualified to bring the reader to a fuller understanding of low temperature work. He has assembled a wealth of methods, procedures, and directions to assist those who wish to broaden their concepts, perhaps to enjoy new adventures in ceramics.

Leon Nigrosh, in a clear and sensible manner, encourages the users of this book to experiment and record results so they can express their ideas knowledgeably, in products of excellence. Many potters, faced with rising fuel costs, find it imperative to review and modify their methods of production. *Low Fire* offers valuable information toward possible solutions to such practical matters, as well as to broader technical and aesthetic considerations.

Lyle N. Perkins, Ph.D.
Professor, Ceramics and Glassblowing
Art Department
University of Massachusetts

Acknowledgments

My thanks to all the clayworkers who offered pictures for consideration, particularly those whose work is shown along with the techniques presented in this book. I am also indebted to those people who have allowed me to share technical information about their clays, glazes, and firing procedures. William Alexander, Harriet Brisson, Shelley Cushner, and Robert Silverman each deserve thanks for their help on different aspects of primitive firing. David Davison's day-long demonstration on soda-raku and vapor firing was enlightening. Paul Soldner's thirty-minute tape about salt bisque was a welcome correspondence. My gratitude goes to Kurt Wild and gracemarie Hanson for their insights on kiln building. Thanks also to Pamela Vandiver for sharing her expertise in Egyptian paste.

A particular note of appreciation goes to Jack Russell for his darkroom magic in preparing many of the photographs for this book. Bill Byers, too.

The staff at Davis Publications deserves recognition for their enthusiasm and support throughout this venture.

And once again, I am especially grateful to my wife, Gale, for finding time to lend her invaluable inspiration and editing skills while pursuing her own career.

LIN

Introduction

This book presents low temperature firing methods and decorating techniques as approaches to designing and working in clay. Along with many new ideas, it attempts to organize information which has been discussed in bits and pieces elsewhere. The simplest methods, using relatively crude procedures at the lowest temperatures, are shown first. More complex methods, using more sophisticated equipment at higher temperatures, are explained later. It is assumed that readers are familiar with basic clay forming techniques and have some understanding of the glazing and firing of ceramic ware.

This is not an alternative energy manual for potters. It is an attempt to develop an awareness of and appreciation for historical and contemporary low fire ceramic processes. Aside from whatever energy may be saved, each technique has its own inherent aesthetic to be sought out, defined, worked with, and admired. The great attachment in this country to high fire stoneware has relegated many low fire objects to the level of bric-a-brac simply because they do not fit the current taste. The purpose of this book is not to re-create Ming porcelains with low fire ware, but to help people recognize the artistic qualities of low fire itself.

For thousands of years, from the smoldering cook fires of the Mesolithic era to the roaring blast furnaces of today, mastering the power of fire to transform substances has been a continual challenge. But just as the discoveries of modern pyrotechnology have begun to filter down from industry to studio potters, we find ourselves beset by an increasing energy shortage. Just as we have begun to use techniques of kiln design to reach and sustain high temperatures, we are told of dwindling supplies and increasing costs of gas for our kilns.

One approach to the problem is to increase the efficiency of existing kilns and to develop new types of kilns that incorporate space age insulating materials, electronic monitoring devices, heat feedback systems, and alternative sources of heat. However, this approach creates a problem. The technology that enables us to use high temperatures separates the potter from much of the joy and experimentation of the earlier, low temperature firing processes. By directly witnessing the changes that take place when low heat is applied to clay and glaze, the mysteries of the ceramic process are revealed.

An end to high fire ceramics is certainly not foreseen here, nor is it desired. It is hoped that this book will make a wider range of knowledge and choice available to clayworkers, so that they might broaden their enjoyment in producing a more varied selection of wares. Clayworkers, as all artists, are not only dependent upon the public's appreciation of their work, but they must also continue to show the public new works to appreciate.

Chapter 1

UNFIRED CLAY

Some clayworkers consider their objects made of unfired clay to be complete. They feel that firing would in some way alter the artistic statement. Works of this type are often purposely left exposed to natural elements. This exposure will eventually return the clay to its original condition. In fact, decomposition is what happens to all unprotected, raw clay objects.

ADOBE

Ware that has been fired to the lowest possible temperature is sun-baked earth — adobe. It has been used as a major building material for centuries by many cultures all over the world and is still used today in many dry and semidry climates. Some clayworkers and sculptors are now turning to adobe for its aesthetic possibilities. Because actual firing is not necessary, massive outdoor structures can be built without being limited by kiln size.

Certain soils are better for making adobe than others. Soil with high kaolin content is best. Kaolin does not *hydrate,* or take on water, and expand as easily as other clays. Therefore, it makes the adobe less likely to crack when it is drying. The soil should also contain fairly coarse sand. Beach sand is not acceptable because the salt content can prevent good adhesion, weakening the adobe.

To determine if local soil is suitable for adobe, a few simple tests should be performed. Dig and dry a soil sample. Sift out pebbles and unwanted organic materials through a window screen. Take a handful of the soil, put it in a jar of water and shake it until it is thoroughly mixed. Let the mixture settle until the water becomes clear. The clay content should be between 25 and 45 percent of the mixture; sand

1-1

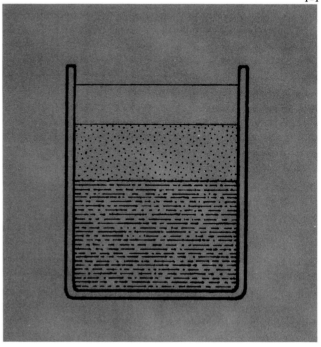

1–1 Test jar: section

1–2 John Goodheart
Axial Plane, 1977
Wet clay, wood, rope
3 x 4 x 60 feet (.9 x 1.2 x 18.1 m)

1–3 Wampanoag Indian
Pots, c. 1899
Unfired clay; wheel thrown
Tallest: 7¾ inches (19.7 cm)
Courtesy: National Museum of Natural
History, Smithsonian Institution

1–2
1–3

1-4 Joyce Kohl
Adobe Form, 1978
Stabilized adobe; paddled
4 x 5 x 4 feet (1.2 x 1.5 x 1.2 m)

and silt should be between 50 and 75 percent. Too much clay will cause the adobe to shrink excessively and crack upon drying. Too much sand and silt will cause the adobe to be crumbly. If the soil is found to be too high in sand or clay content after testing, add whichever ingredient is necessary to achieve the desired balance. Chopped straw can be added in amounts of up to 10 percent to cut shrinkage and open adobe that has a high clay content.

The problem with traditional adobe is that it is not waterproof and requires continual repairs and patching. However, adobe can be made waterproof by adding stabilizers such as pitch, glues, or cements. The stabilizer most recommended by artists and the Uniform Building Code Standards is emulsified asphalt. Emulsified asphalt is a viscous mixture of tiny droplets of asphalt suspended in water. This material is generally available, under different brand

1-4

1-5 Bruce Wood
Form, 1977
Stabilized adobe, straw; press molded
Diameter: 18 inches (45.7 cm)

1-6 Dale Gaynor
Yucca Bubbles, 1973
Stabilized adobe, burlap, yucca; draped
42 x 15 x 4 inches (106.7 x 38.1 x 10.2 cm)

1-5

1-6

names, through local paving contractors or oil dealers. It should be stored in a warm place above 10°C (50°F) so that the asphalt does not congeal and settle.

Because clay has greater absorbency than the other materials in adobe, the emulsified asphalt is drawn to the particles of clay and encases them. This makes the clay, and therefore the adobe, impervious to water.

To test for the proper amount of stabilizer, mix several 1000 gram (g) batches of soil, each with sufficient water to reach a workable consistency. Add the emulsified asphalt in additions from 1 to 6 percent. Mix thoroughly and form into small bricks. Allow the samples to dry away from direct sun for at least twenty-four hours. Samples can be dried in a warm oven at about 65°C (150°F) with the door ajar.

When the samples have dried completely, try to break each one in half. The best sample is one that will not crumble, but will break with sharp edges. To find which sample is most waterproof, immerse them in separate containers of water for several hours. A properly stabilized sample will not cloud the water and will show no softening of its edges. Choose the sample with the least amount of emulsified asphalt required to fully stabilize the soil. When the adobe has reached stabilization, additional asphalt has no effect.

Once the proper mixture has been determined,

larger quantities of soil, straw, water, and emulsified asphalt can be mixed to a consistency suitable for working.

Portland cement in amounts of up to 20 percent can be used as a stabilizer instead of emulsified asphalt, The adobe may be stronger, but because the cement does not encase the clay particles, it will not be as waterproof.

If satisfactory adobe soil is not available, reasonable facsimiles can be mixed in the studio. The following formulas have been developed by Bill Gilbert:

Adobe for Small Hand Building:

Sand (sifted through window screen)	55
Coarse Fireclay	30
Red Earthenware	10
Red Iron Oxide	5
	100

Adobe for Large Sculpture:

Coarse Sand (20-mesh or larger)	50
Fireclay	30
Red Iron Oxide	5
Fine Sand or Soil	15
	100

Adobe can be put into press molds or laid over drape molds. It can be shoveled into a heap, paddled, carved, or otherwise worked into a finished form. For large pieces, a wood and wire framework can be used as an armature.

Adobe objects, like work made of other clays, should be allowed to set up and dry slowly, either by occasionally spraying them with a light mist of water or by covering them with plastic. This will help reduce the possibility of the adobe cracking as it dries.

Chapter 2

CHOOSING A CLAY

Prospecting for local clay can be good preparation, both materially and mentally, for primitive firings. After all, early potters were not able to phone in their clay orders.

Workable clay is most easily found at riverbanks, road cuts, quarries, or building sites where the *overburden,* or soil cover, has already been removed. To obtain maps which would indicate clay deposits, contact a local office of the United States Department of Agriculture and ask for a soil map. These maps note soil conditions only to a depth of one meter (39.37 inches). State and county geological surveys may have maps showing clay deposits at greater depths. Information can also be obtained from:

The National Cartographic Information Center
U.S. Geological Survey
507 National Center
Reston, Virginia 22092

In Canada, contact:

Department of Energy, Mines, and Resources
Survey and Mapping Branch
615 Booth Street
Ottawa, Ontario, Canada K1A OE9

ON-SITE TESTS

Simple on-site tests will determine if the clay can be used successfully to make objects. First, wet the clay just enough to make a small plastic ball. Roll it into a pencil-thick coil and wrap it around a finger. If the coil shows few cracks, the clay is reasonably plastic. Next, allow a piece of wet clay to dry. If a whitish scum forms, the clay contains alkalies. While certain alkalies may be beneficial to high temperature clays and glazes, at low temperatures soluble alkalies often cause a white scum on the surface of the fired clay. Worse, alkalies may also reduce the plasticity of the clay, flux the clay too much, and cause the ware to slump when fired. If alkalies are present, they can be easily removed during the washing stage of the clay preparation.

If the clay contains lime, it may not be suitable for firing, especially at low temperatures. Free lime particles hydrate, which causes them to expand after firing and pop craters in the fired object. To test for lime, drop a small sample of the clay into a 50 percent solution of hydrochloric acid. If bubbling occurs, an excess of lime is present.

Sand, mineral fragments, and organic materials can usually be screened from the clays. However, if it appears that removing these impurities will require more effort than it is worth, find another clay deposit.

PREPARING THE CLAY

If the clay passes all the tests, dig at least a 5 pound (2.27 kg) sample from the vein, break it into small pieces and allow it to dry. Crush the clay and screen it through a 60-mesh sieve to remove granular impurities. Then, pour the clay into a container of water and stir vigorously. After a few hours, siphon, rather than pour off, the dirty top water. This removes the alkalies and organic matter without losing any of the fine clay particles. Add more water, stir, allow the clay to settle, and siphon again. Repeat this process until the water is clear. Then siphon off all the water and pour the clay onto a clean floor, wooden boards, or plaster bats. Leave the clay exposed to the air until it is almost stiff. Roll most of the clay into a ball and store it in an airtight container such as a plastic bag or a bucket with a snap-lock cover. Allow the sample to *temper,* or age, for at least a week to improve plasticity. When the remaining portion of the sample has dried completely, crush and screen it again so that it can be tested further.

Although the following tests may be more important for clays that are fired closer to vitrification than those that are primitive fired, it is still worth the effort to discover as much as possible about the properties of any clay in order to use it effectively.

WATER OF PLASTICITY

To determine *water of plasticity,* or the amount of water needed to bring the clay to a workable consistency, fill a 100 cubic centimenter (cc) graduated cylinder with water. Add only enough water into 100 g of dry powdered clay to make the mixture plastic. Record the amount of water used. Add more water until the clay is sticky. Record this additional amount. This test gives the range of water content needed to make the clay workable. The number of cubic centimeters of water equals the percentage of water of plasticity. (One cc of water weighs one g.)

SHRINKAGE

To test for shrinkage, make some clay bars 13 centimeters (cm) long, 4 cm wide, and 1 cm thick. Draw a line 10 cm long on each bar. Sandwich the bars between light plaster bats or plywood boards to avoid warping during the drying process. When the clay has completely dried, measure each line with a centimeter ruler. The number of millimeters each bar has shrunk equals its percentage of dry shrinkage. Fire the bars and measure again. The additional shrinkage is the percentage of fired shrinkage. The total shrinkage is the sum of both the dry and fired shrinkage.

POROSITY

To test for *porosity,* an indication of clay vitrification, separately weigh several unglazed fired samples of the clay. Boil them in water for at least two hours. Remove the samples, blot them, and immediately weigh each of them again. Absorption is calculated as follows:

$$\frac{\text{Saturated Weight} - \text{Dry Weight}}{\text{Dry Weight}} \times 100 = \frac{\text{Percentage}}{\text{Absorption}}$$

Fire additional samples to a range of different temperatures and repeat these tests. The combination of shrinkage and porosity information helps determine the best firing temperature for the particular clay.

Natural shrinkage rates vary from 10 to 25 percent,

with 12 to 15 percent considered good. The porosity or absorption rate for earthenware is usually 4 to 10 percent.

If the clay samples test satisfactorily, dig a sufficiently large quantity to help ensure consistency in the clay body over a period of time. Prepare the clay properly and store it for later use.

CLAY BODIES

It is possible to use some clays directly to make objects for primitive firing. However, many natural earthenware clays are fine grained and are too compact to withstand the vagaries of the fire. Opening the structure of the clay body will help ensure against cracks and explosions. This can be done by adding sand, grog, volcanic ash (pumice), or other nonplastic fillers. As much as 50 percent addition of these fillers, alone or in combination, can be used. The clay will be easier to work, will shrink and warp less, and will better withstand the thermal shock of the fire. Fireclays can be added for color, texture, and additional strength.

Commercial earthenware or whiteware bodies can often be used in primitive firings, but should be tested for suitability before any modifications are made. Stoneware and porcelain clay bodies, because they are quite refractory, can often be used in primitive firing with little or no filler additions.

PRIMITIVE FIRE CLAY BODIES

Kurt Wild's

Talc (TOM)	6.8
Ball Clay (OM#4)	6.2
Cedar Heights Redart	31.5
Cedar Heights Goldart	16.0
Fireclay (Kaiser)	23.5
Silica Sand (55-mesh)	16.0

Amerindian

Local Clay	50
Volcanic Ash (Pumice)	50

Robert Silverman's

Fireclay	40
Cedar Heights Redart	20
Volcanic Ash (Pumice)	15
Grog (40/80 mesh)	15
Talc	10
Bentonite	1

Roberta Marks's

Ocmulgee (Georgia red clay)	100
Ball Clay	15
Medium Grog	20

Chapter 3

PRIMITIVE FIRING

ON-GROUND FIRING

The earliest known clay firings were done directly on the ground. A few precautions are necessary when using this method. Fire on a day with little or no breeze. Clear the ground of all flammable material at least 6 feet (1.8 m) wide around the fire. Buckets of water or a garden hose should be ready in case of an emergency.

Set a manageable pile of fuel, such as dried twigs, corncobs, or dung, in the center of the cleared area. Place the dried clay ware around the pile. Carefully ignite the fuel. When the fire has burned to a bed of coals, put the warmed ware onto the coals using sticks or tongs. Place the ware upside down to ensure even heating. Add more fuel but do not smother the ware. Continue to add fuel until the ware appears to have *sintered,* that is, darkened and changed from a soft to a hard state. This may take from thirty minutes to four or more hours depending upon the heat of the fire, the type of clay, and the size and number of pieces being fired. If the ware is to retain oxidation colors, simply allow the fire to die out. For reduction effects, completely cover the ware with fuel near the end of the firing and let it slowly burn down.

The temperature reached with this type of firing is around cone 022 (585°C/1085°F), sufficiently past the temperature at which the chemically combined water has begun to evaporate from the clay.

3-1 Chiapas, Mexico
Street firing
Photo: C. David Hiser

3-2 Ware warming around open pit

3-3 Mandan, Dakota
Vessel, c. 1868
Earthenware; cord impressions, hand built
Courtesy: National Museum of Natural
   History, Smithsonian Institution
Gift of Dr. C. C. Gray

Results from on-ground firing are the least predictable among low fire procedures. Heating is bound to be uneven and large numbers of pieces will probably not survive the fire.

OPEN PIT FIRING

The quality of ware fired in an open pit is noticeably better than ware fired on the ground. Because the walls of the pit help to contain the fire and act as insulation, an open pit can be considered a very rudimentary kiln. A typical pit might be from 16 to 30 inches (40.6 to 76.2 cm) deep, 3 to 5 feet (.9 to 1.5 m) in length and about 2 or 3 feet (.6 to .9 m) wide. Size can best be determined by the available space, how much ware is to be fired, and how much one feels like digging. The earth that is dug from the pit can be used to make a mound around the rim of the pit for added depth and insulation.

To fire this kiln, place fuel, such as kindling, dried corncobs, or dung, on the bottom and along the sides of the pit. Closely pack dry ware in the pit. Fuel can be placed in and between the ware. Put a layer of fuel on top of the entire setting. Ignite the fuel from the top and allow it to burn slowly. This will help ensure that the ware is thoroughly dry. Because air cannot pass easily through the fuel into the pit, temperature rise is usually not too rapid. As the fuel burns down and a bed of coals is formed, add more fuel until the fire has built up above the rim of the pit. Continue this process until the ware has reached a glowing red heat. If the fire is allowed to simply die out, the ware will have oxidation colors. For reduction, wet leaves or straw, ashes, or dry powdered dung can be used to cover the entire pit while the ware is still hot. The ware should not be touched until all of the embers have died out.

A well-managed pit fire can reach temperatures

3-2

3-3

3-4 Harrapa (Pakistan)
Painted jar, prehistoric
Earthenware; hand built
21$\frac{3}{4}$ x 19$\frac{1}{2}$ inches (55.2 x 49.5 cm)
Courtesy: Museum of Fine Arts, Boston
  Harvard-MFA Expedition

3-4

3-5 Covered pit kiln: section

from cone 018 to cone 09 (696° to 915°C/1285° to 1679°F). The result will be pieces that are reasonably sturdy but, because they have not vitrified, are still quite porous.

COVERED PIT FIRING

Firings in covered pits attain higher temperatures than open fires, producing ware that is less fragile.

Again, the size of the pit depends on practical considerations. However, if the long side of the pit runs in the direction of the prevailing breeze, the pit will gain higher temperatures because of the improved air/fuel mixture.

To construct this type of kiln, the windward, or front, end of the pit should be tapered toward ground level, while the sides of the pit wall should be steep. Place small pieces of wood in the bottom and along the sides of the pit. Set warm, dry ware on the fuel up to about one-quarter of the distance from the front. Cover the pit with corrugated sheet metal, or some other sturdy nonflammable material. Leave a small opening at the rear to act as a flue

3–6
3–5

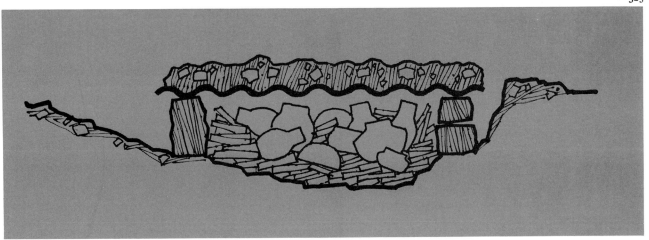

3-7 Pi Benio
Steam Iron
Bisque fired porcelain, cloth, leaves,
    pine needles; thrown, slab, hand built
Each iron: 21 x 22 x 14 inches
    (53.3 x 55.9 x 35.6 cm)
Photo: Roman Sapecki

3-8 Pi Benio
Blimp in Hangar
Bisque fired porcelain, electrical cord,
    coathanger; thrown, hand built
17 x 11 inches (43.2 x 27.9 cm)

and a larger opening at the front for the firemouth. The sheet metal should be covered with earth for added insulation.

Ignite the fuel in the pit. When it has burned to coals, add more fuel through the firemouth. By continuing this process, particularly if pieces of wood 1 to 2 inches (2.5 to 5.1 cm) in diameter are used, cone 05 (1031°C/1888°F) or higher can be reached in a few hours.

For oxidation effects, the firemouth is only partially closed with bricks or stones and the flue is left open until the fire dies out completely. Do not use damp bricks or stones as the heat of the fire might cause them to explode.

To reduce the clay, the firemouth should be closed almost completely between stokings, allowing only enough air to ensure continued burning. At the end of the fire, both the firemouth and the flue should be closed to prevent the ware from reoxidizing.

3-7
3-8

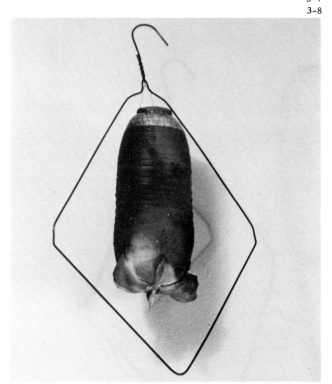

SHEET METAL BOX FIRING

Some members of Southwest Native American tribes utilize a sheet metal box as the ware chamber in another closed kiln firing method. First, clear the ground and dig a very shallow pit. Place four to six large tin cans upright in the pit. These will act as legs to elevate the ware chamber. Place tinder and kindling around and between the cans. Put the bottom of the sheet metal box on top of the cans. Set the dry ware in the box and tightly cover it with the lid. Wire grill laid on the floor of the empty box can protect the ware from sudden heat changes. Place dried cow manure pies around and over the box. Stack split pieces of wood around the whole mound. Ignite the tinder on all sides. The fire should burn for at least an hour, and will reach cone 015 (790°C/1454°F) or higher.

3-9 Rio Grande Pueblo Canteen, c. 1938
Earthenware, slip, woven cotton; hand
  built, burnished
Diameter: 8 inches (20.3 cm)
Courtesy: National Museum of Natural
  History, Smithsonian Institution
Gift of Mrs. Marcus Benjamin

3-10 Setting pottery into box
Photo: Shelley Cushner

3-11 Placing cow manure around
  covered box
Photo: Shelley Cushner

3-12 Firing in progress
Photo: Shelley Cushner

3-10

3-11   3-12

3-9

3-13 Fireclay kiln: section

To reduce the ware, the stacking and firing procedure is the same. When the fire is burning strongly, smother the entire mound with dry, crumbled manure and then let the fire die out. Traditionally, horse manure is used for reduction, but any easily crumbled manure will do. For best results, it is important that no smoke escape from the fire.

A major advantage of this primitive firing method is that the ware is protected from breakage caused by shifting fuel.

Although not traditionally done, it is possible to use very low temperature glazes on ware fired in this manner.

If natural cow manure is not readily available, artificial dung which smolders and heats like the real thing may be made. Mix one part wheat paste, two parts ball clay, and enough water to form a slurry. Add medium sawdust until the mixture is crumbly. Pat large handfuls of it into pies and let them dry thoroughly before use.

FIRECLAY KILN

A crude, but effective, updraft wood-fired kiln with twin fireboxes can be constructed and fired within a few hours. The only materials needed are two pieces of stovepipe 36 inches (91.4 cm) long and 10 inches (25.4 cm) in diameter, some heavy plastic sheet, and 150 pounds (68 kg) of a mixture of equal parts fireclay and chopped straw.

To build the kiln, dig an 8 foot (2.4 m) round-bottomed trench a foot (30.5 cm) wide and 5 inches (12.7 cm) deep. In the center of the trench, dig a circular depression 18 inches (45.7 cm) wide and 4 inches (10.2 cm) deeper. This area will be the floor of the ware chamber. Next, construct the firing rack to hold the ware. On a wooden board, using the fireclay and straw mixture, make a slab 15 to 16 inches (38.1 to 40.6 cm) in diameter. Attach a number of coils lengthwise on the slab to form a series of

3-13

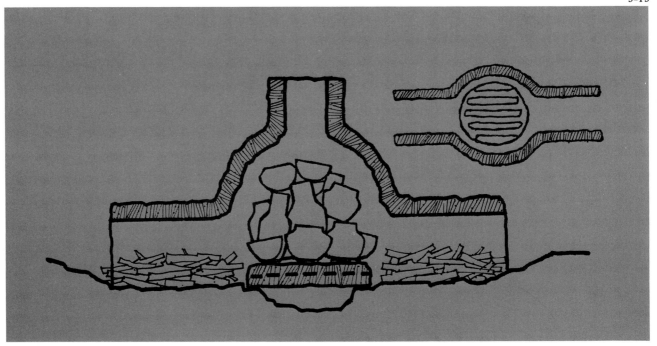

3-14 Constructing fireboxes
Photo: gracemarie Hanson

3-15 Constructing ware chamber
Photo: gracemarie Hanson

3-16 Firing the kiln
Photo: gracemarie Hanson

3-14

3-15

3-16

furrows 2 inches (5.1 cm) deep. While the rack is stiffening, the fireboxes may be constructed. Place the stovepipes in both ends of the trench and lay the plastic over them. Pack 2 to 3 inches (5.1 to 7.6 cm) of clay on top of the plastic over the entire length of the pipe. When the rack has stiffened, slide it from the board into the ware chamber area. Then construct a combination chamber and stack by fashioning 2 to 3 inch (5.1 to 7.6 cm) coils into a widemouthed bottle shape about 30 inches (76.2 cm) tall. During the construction, dry fireclay should be sprinkled on the coils to aid in stiffening the clay. After the stack is finished and the clay is allowed to harden somewhat, the stovepipes should be carefully pulled out. It is not necessary to remove the

plastic, because it will burn out during the early stages of the firing. Gently set unglazed pots in the ware chamber through the stack. Pieces can be set on top of others to fill the chamber halfway up.

To dry the kiln, start a very small fire in both fireboxes and keep them burning for at least a half hour. When the clay has dried, introduce sticks of wood about 1 inch (2.4 cm) in diameter and 12 inches (30.5 cm) long into both fireboxes to bring up the temperature slowly. Continue to add more wood at an increasing pace until flame leaps out of the stack to a height of about 2 feet (.6 m). Keep the flame in this attitude for at least an hour. It is important that both fireboxes be stoked at the same time. Otherwise, the draft might fail, the flame

3-17 Double drum kiln: section

3-18 Triple drum kiln: section

3-18

3-17

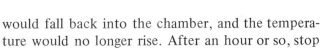

would fall back into the chamber, and the temperature would no longer rise. After an hour or so, stop stoking and let the fire go out. When the kiln has cooled, the ware can be removed with tongs.

A firing in this kiln will produce good, hard, partially reduced bisqued ware. It is possible to reach temperatures near cone 02 (1100°C/2012°F).

DRUM KILN

Drawn by the appeal of primitive fired objects, but looking for more predictable results, ceramist Kurt Wild has developed what he calls "a sort of twentieth

3-19 Triple drum kiln without cover on second drum
Photo: Kurt Wild

3-20 Kurt Wild
Blackware pots
Earthenware, slip; hand built, burnished
Tallest: 9¾ inches (24.8 cm)
Collection: the artist
Photo: Jens Gunelson

3-19

century primitive" approach to his own work. Based on early pit fire techniques, he has built and successfully used a double drum kiln. The outer drum acts as a chimney, which draws air to the fuel, and also as a retaining wall which keeps the fuel next to the inner drum where it is needed.

The outer shell is a 55 gallon (208 L) drum with top and bottom removed. The ware chamber is a 15 gallon (56.8 L) drum with only the top removed. Place each drum on three vertically standing bricks. Put 2 inches (5.1 cm) of sand on the floor of the smaller drum to insulate pots from a sudden heat increase. If it is windy, erect a windscreen of con-

3-20

4-1 Roberta B. Marks
Vessel
Earthenware; coil, slab built, burnished
20 x 17 inches (50.8 x 43.2 cm)
Photo: Marlyse Divernois

crete blocks or stones about 1 foot (30.5 cm) from the base of the kiln.

Start a small wood fire under the drums. When the fire has turned to glowing embers, almost fill the inner drum by carefully placing the pots one on top of another. Keep a small fire for at least an hour to heat the ware through the water smoking stage. Add more wood from underneath to increase the heat. Then drop more wood between the walls of the two drums. Keep the fire raging for at least a half hour. For oxidation effects, let the fire die out. To bring about reduction, after the flames have died down, dump sawdust into the smaller drum completely covering the pots. Place a lid over the drum and allow the fire to go out.

Because Wild's work is highly decorated, he became concerned about blemishes and shiny spots produced by the sawdust dumped directly onto the pots. To solve this problem, he devised a triple drum setting.

The innermost can and its cover have closely spaced, small holes drilled or punched all around. The second drum is a 15 gallon (56.8 L) drum with the top removed and cut to a height of 17½ inches (44.5 cm). The outer shell is a 55 gallon (208 L) drum with the bottom and top removed and the top third cut off.

Place ware in the innermost can and put on the lid. The firing then proceeds the same way as in the double drum setting. When it is time to reduce the ware, pour sawdust into the second drum and put on its lid. The innermost can protects the ware from the sawdust while still allowing the smoke to thoroughly penetrate the ware.

Chapter 4

SAWDUST FIRING

Sawdust firing heats and hardens clay using a simple kiln. This firing technique is somewhat less harsh on clay objects than pit firing. Temperature buildup is more gradual and the normal cooling period takes longer than most pit fires. Because of this, extended forms, such as wide, shallow bowls, narrow-necked vases, and forms with appendages, can be fired with greater likelihood of survival. Hand built or wheel thrown pieces may be fired with this method if they have thin, even walls. Almost any kind of open clay body can be used to make objects for sawdust firing.

A good sawdust firing brings about natural reduction on unglazed ware. Burnished or unburnished slip, and carved or incised decorations adapt well to this type of firing. Because of the direct contact of the sawdust on both the interior and exterior of the ware, the use of glaze is not recommended.

After the objects have been made, they should be allowed to dry completely before they are placed in the kiln. Warming or sun-baking them just prior to stacking will help ensure that most of the atmospheric moisture has been driven out.

Some clayworkers prefer to bisque fire their ware before putting it in a sawdust fire. This is not necessary, with the exception of pieces that are very large or in which a great deal of time has been invested in decoration.

Most clays will turn black in a sawdust fire because of carbonization. However, previously bisqued ware

4–2 Joan Daub
Pot
Bisque fired stoneware; coil built, burnished
11 x 14 inches (27.9 x 35.6 cm)

4–3 Barbara Shaiman
Inside/Outside #15
Bisque fired stoneware; hand built, burnished
6 x 5½ x 12 inches (15.2 x 14 x 30.1 cm)
Photo: Steve Voorheis

4–2
4–3

will be more durable and can also offer different color effects. If red or buff clays are bisqued, they will not become completely black. Colored slips applied to leather hard objects which are then bisqued before firing tend to retain more color. When used in this manner, copper carbonate offers a wide range of color, including pinks and reds.

It is also possible to sawdust fire glazed ware that has been previously fired to stoneware temperatures. This can bring about interesting carbon clouding and crackle effects.

Steven J. Howell
Basket
Terra cotta, slip; slab built; sawdust fired
7 x 15 inches (17.8 x 38.1 cm)
Photo: Peter Moriarty

Author
Globe vase, 1979
High fired porcelain, glaze, luster; thrown
6 x 6 inches (15.2 x 15.2 cm)

Robert Silverman
Bottle, 1978
Earthenware; coil-thrown, burnished; pit fired
Height: 23 inches (58.4 cm)

William C. Alexander
Footed Pot
(Photographed to show underside)
Hollow rim contains rattle
Earthenware, terra sigillata; thrown, press molded
4 x 14 inches (10.2 x 35.6 cm)
Photo: Mark Eichinger

Bill Gilbert
Blanket, 1977
Adobe, wood, wire mesh; hand formed; air dried
8 x 5 x 12 feet (2.4 x 1.5 x 3.7 m)

David Davison
Form, 1978
Porcelain; thrown, altered; vapor glazed
16 x 11 inches (40.6 x 27.9 cm)

Kurt Weiser
Raku Jar
Raku clay, glaze; thrown, hand built
17 x 12 inches (43.2 x 30.1 cm)

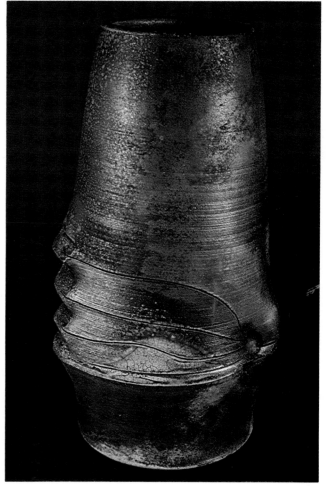

Gina L. Halpern
Sir Bascombe Hargreaves III, 1973
Three drawers in back contain tea set
Clay, underglaze; slab, hand built
26 x 18 inches (66 x 45.7 cm)
Collection: Mo Septee

Jan Havens
Bird
High fired stoneware, nonfired ceramic stain,
  acrylic paint finish; hand built
Height: 23 inches (58.4 cm)
Photo: Barry Havens

Bill Stewart
Alligator Woman with Trained Snakes and Bugs, 1978
White earthenware, underglaze, glaze, luster; hand built
Height: 30 inches (76.2 cm)

Toby Buonagurio
Robot #5, 1977–78
Clay, glaze, luster, acrylic paint, glitter,
  flocking; slip cast, hand built
Height: 18 inches (45.7 cm)

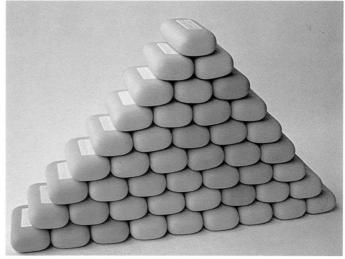

Karen Thuesen Massaro
Alla Glicerina, 1975
White clay, underglaze; slip cast
18 x 18 x 3½ inches (45.7 x 45.7 x 8.9 cm)

Beverley Kurtz Magennis
The Only House with an Apple Tree, 1976
Talc clay, glaze; slab built
26 x 48 x 13 inches (66 x 122 x 33 cm)

Helaine Ettinger
Basket
Terra cotta; thrown, hand built; majolica glaze
Height: 14 inches (35.6 cm)

Louis Marak
Portal Bowl
White earthenware, underglaze, underglaze pencil, decal,
  glaze, luster; slip cast, slab, extruded
5 x 11 x 10 inches (12.7 x 27.9 x 25.4 cm)

Blair J. Lariviere
Garden of Eden, 1978
High fired stoneware, glaze, luster; thrown, excised
9½ x 7½ inches (24.1 x 14 cm)
Photo: Joseph O. Thibodeau

Jens Art Morrison
*Entering the Tower of Flight (Astro-Altar, Late
    Farmounian),* 1978
Talc clay, river clay, stains, luster; hand built
Height: 18 inches (45.7 cm)
Photo: Sharon Osa Oliver

Dan Gunderson
Cone, 1979
White earthenware, underglaze, glaze, china paint; thrown
Height: 34 inches (86.1 cm)
Photo: Brenda Gunderson

Robert Palusky
Vase, 1977
Talc clay, colored clay, underglaze pencil, glaze, luster;
    thrown, hand built
15 x 7 inches (38.1 x 17.8 cm)

Douglas Fey
Plate
Earthenware, slip, glaze; thrown
Diameter: 16 inches (40.6 cm)

Paul Bérubé
Platter, 1979
High fired stoneware, engobe, glaze, Picceramic
    process, overglaze enamel, luster; thrown
    sgraffito
Diameter: 19 inches (48.1 cm)

Susan and Steven Kemenyffy
Rock-Hard Beverly
Raku clay, glaze, luster; slab built, incised
24 x 22 inches (61 x 55.9 cm)

Author
Spirit of '76 Drum Cookie Jar, 1976
High fired porcelain, glaze, decal, china paint,
    luster; slab built
8 x 7½ inches (20.3 x 19.1 cm)

4-4 Tom Neugebauer
Remains II, 1978
Bisque fired stoneware, charred beam;
   thrown, stretched, hand built
16 x 16 inches (40.6 x 40.6 cm)

4-5 Gretchen Stevens Cochran
Peach Baskets, 1976
Earthenware; slip cast, hand formed
Each: 20 x 14 inches (50.8 x 35.6 cm)

4-6 Chuck Flagg
Reliquary-Form II
Terra cotta, slip; thrown, coil, slab built
18 x 9 x 8 inches (45.7 x 22.9 x
   20.3 cm)

4-4   4-5   4-6

SAWDUST

There are divergent opinions on which type of sawdust is best for firing. Some people feel that superior effects can be brought about by using only exotic woods, while others are more concerned about the size of sawdust particles. Experiment with different types of wood and note the variations for further use. Sawdust that is very fine will burn too quickly and could possibly explode into flame when ignited. Coarse, rough-cut sawdust leaves too many air spaces for adequate reduction. The most consistent results can usually be obtained from a mixture of 70 percent medium and 30 percent coarse sawdust. Small amounts of bench shavings can also be mixed with sawdust. In all cases, the sawdust should be dry to afford complete burning.

LOOSE BRICK KILN

Sawdust firing makes good use of materials otherwise considered as waste: sawdust and used brick.

Different sizes and shapes of kilns can be easily constructed because no mortar is necessary. The construction and packing of the kiln should be done outdoors and both can be done at the same time.

Use an area of cleared, flat ground as the kiln floor. Set the first course of bricks as the perimeter of the floor. Because not much insulation is needed, the bricks can be set on edge rather than on face. This also means that fewer bricks are needed to gain the full height of the kiln. Place the bricks together fairly tightly. However, some passage of air is necessary to ensure complete combustion during the fire.

After two courses of brick have been set up, pour in 4 to 6 inches (10.2 to 15.2 cm) of sawdust and tamp it evenly across the whole floor. Place a few of the heaviest objects on this base. For equal heating during the fire, fill the ware with sawdust. Add more brick courses. Then pour more sawdust around and over the pieces, tamping lightly, until the ware is completely covered. Add another course of bricks and then pour in 3 to 4 inches (7.6 to 10.2 cm) of sawdust and tamp. Continue to place more objects in the same manner until the kiln is completed. Shallow bowls and plates should be packed on edge to reduce breakage. Fill bottle shapes to the top with sawdust and place them right side up to ensure proper heating from within as well as from the outside.

The kiln should not be filled with more than three layers of ware. As the fire progresses, the sawdust cushion burns away and all the pots end up on top of one another on the floor of the kiln. Too much weight will break those pieces on the bottom of the pile.

When the kiln is packed, add one more brick course and then place tightly bunched newspaper on top of the sawdust to act as tinder. Light the paper with a long fireplace match. Be sure all the paper is burning before the kiln is covered. In the kiln shown here, a galvanized trash can lid serves as an ideal

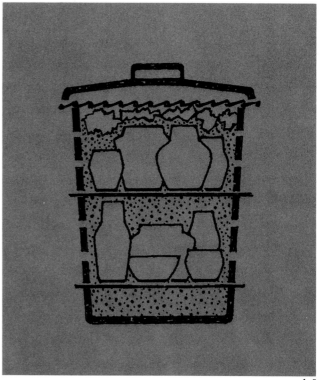

4-8

4-7

cover, leaving small openings at the corners to allow air in and smoke out. Larger diameter kilns will require sheet metal or asbestos board covers. Once the fire has been started, do not handle the cover until all smoking has ceased and everything has cooled.

The length of time needed to complete a firing depends on several factors: the size of the kiln, what kind of sawdust is used, how tightly the kiln is packed, and how much air can get in to aid combustion. Firings can take from three or four hours to three or four days.

If the bricks are set too tightly, not enough air can get in and the kiln could smolder for days. Bricks set too loosely will cause the kiln to burn too fast, preventing adequate heating and good reduction. Experimenting with the placement and size of the air spaces can bring about interesting flashes of iridescence on some of the fired pots while still providing good overall reduction.

TRASH CAN KILN

Another type of sawdust kiln can be made from a galvanized trash can. Drill or punch small holes at random all over the can to allow adequate air intake. Pack and fire this kiln in the same manner as a brick kiln. If after test firing the kiln it is found to have too few holes, more can be punched. If there are too many holes, some can be easily blocked by inserting roofing nails.

A further refinement can be made by punching an even row of holes at the same height on opposite sides of the can. Small diameter rods such as coat hanger wire can be passed through to form a shelf. This will help prevent the ware from falling as the sawdust burns away.

WATERPROOFING POTS

A sawdust firing will reach between cone 021 and cone 017 (602° to 727°C&1116° to 1341°F). Because these temperatures are not high enough to mature clay, the fired ware will be quite porous. For centuries, people have waterproofed their pots after firing by filling them with milk and allowing them to stand for a few days. Pieces can also be seasoned with cooking oil to reduce the porosity. If necessary, the interior of pots could be coated with liquid acrylic paint to render them waterproof. With either oil or acrylic paint, some of the inherent character of ware fired in sawdust will be lost.

Some clayworkers recommend the use of tung oil to seal primitive and sawdust fired pots. Tung oil, derived from the seeds of the Chinese tung tree, will soak into the porous clay, become hard, leave no shine when it dries, and enhance the quality of the finished piece.

Chapter 5

RAKU

Raku firing as practiced in the United States is so different from traditional Japanese raku that some Japanese potters have objected to the American use of the term. Traditional raku is being done in modern Japan by a direct descendant of Chojiro, who is supposed to be the first potter to have made raku. Following the historical method, a single tea bowl coated with glaze is placed in a clay saggar surrounded by charcoal inside an open topped, circular, clay-walled kiln.

5-1

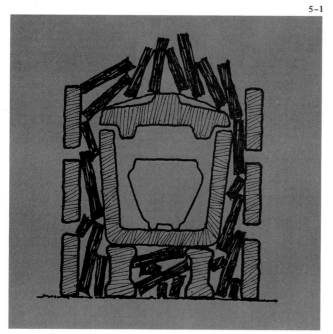

To increase temperature, bits of handpicked charcoal are added slowly. This careful firing may take three or more hours to complete. American clayworkers have developed raku into a relatively inexpensive, fast, and exciting technique. The entire process from wet pot to fired piece can take as little as two hours.

Raku can be done in almost any fuel or electric kiln. A front loading kiln will provide better access for loading and unloading. Long handled metal tongs, asbestos or heavy leather gloves, #2-green welder's goggles, metal water containers, covered metal buckets, and a supply of dry leaves, sawdust, or other combustible material are also needed. A garden hose or fire extinguisher should be handy in case of an emergency.

CLAY

Virtually any clay body that has a sufficient amount of coarse grained clays can be used for raku. Stonewares, porcelains, and high fireclay bodies are particularly good. Adding grog, sand, or sawdust will open the clay body to help withstand the rapid temperature changes.

Pieces to be fired in raku can be made by any forming technique. However, objects with walls that are too thick or too thin, poorly joined parts,

5-1 Japanese raku kiln: section

5-2 Nancy Smith
Container
Bisque fired stoneware; slab built
10 x 4 x 2 inches (25.4 x 10.2 x 5.1 cm)
Photo: the author

5-3 John Goodheart
Raku Cup
Clay, wood; slab built
12 x 6 x 3 inches (30.5 x 15.2 x 7.6 cm)

5-4 Nancee Meeker
Bottle
Earthenware; thrown, etched, unglazed
Height: 15 inches (38.1 cm)
Photo: Jeff Martin (Photographic
    Associates)

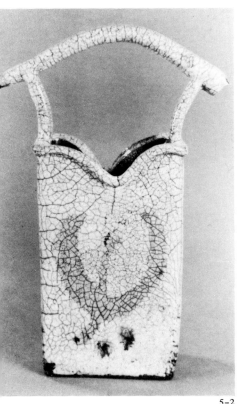

5-2

5-3

5-4

or severely constricted forms can crack or explode when fired.

GLAZE

Raku glazes should have high thermal resistance and should mature rapidly at very low temperatures. Many good raku glazes use lead as the base because of its low melting point and the hard, smooth surface it imparts. However, the fast firing process does not allow enough time for all the lead (and many other chemicals) to fully combine and mature. Extensive use of raku ware for storage of food or drink could therefore cause toxic illness. Bear in mind that because some chemicals may not fully mature, even nonlead-based raku glazes could have a similar effect.

Raku glazes generally mature between cone 022 and cone 08 (585° to 945°C/1085° to 1750°F). This affords the use of a wide range of colorants which normally burn out at higher temperatures. Used alone or in combination, selenium, cadmium, antimony, and chrome can give reds, yellows, and oranges in oxidation. Silver nitrate and stannous chloride can enhance the luster qualities of raku glazes. Copper, when reduced, can give deep reds to shiny, metallic gold colors.

Glazes should be thickly applied and the ware thoroughly dried before firing. Ware should be preheated to prevent the glaze from flaking off moments after being placed in the hot kiln.

5-5 Author
Tea Bowl with Case, 1976
Bisque fired stoneware; hand built
3 x 5 inches (7.6 x 12.7 cm)
Collection: the artist

5-6 Steve Reynolds
Bowl
Raku clay; hand built
5 x 21 x 20 inches (12.7 x 53.3 x
   50.8 cm)

5-7 Arlene Shechet
Under Pressure I
Raku clay, stains; hand built
15 x 15 x 5 inches (38.1 x 38.1 x
   12.7 cm)

FIRING

While it is possible to single fire raku pieces, kiln losses will be decreased if the ware is first bisque fired. To shorten firing time, preheat the empty kiln. Then, wearing gloves and goggles, grasp a pot firmly but carefully with the metal tongs and place it in the kiln. Lift the piece with the tongs from beneath if possible. Otherwise, pick the pot up by inserting one tip of the tongs deep inside and carefully clamping the wall. Do not pick up a piece by the rim because it might break.

Once in the kiln, glazes usually begin to mature within three to thirty minutes, depending upon their composition, the size of the kiln, and the heat advance. Check the firing often by looking into the kiln through the spy hole. When the glaze has stopped bubbling and has become smooth and glossy, use tongs to remove the ware. By allowing a piece to cool in the air or by plunging it immediately into water, oxidation effects can be achieved.

For smoking, or secondary reduction effects, take a pot directly from the kiln with the tongs and place it in a bucket partly filled with combustible material. After the heat of the ware has ignited the material, cover the bucket. Allowing the piece to reduce for five to twenty minutes will produce lustrous glaze effects, bring out reduction colors, and blacken the exposed clay body. Remove the pot from the bucket and either quench it in water or allow it to cool naturally.

BLANKET KILN

With recent advances in industrial insulation materials, many clayworkers have forsaken brick kilns for ones made of ceramic fiber blanket. A relatively inexpensive blanket kiln is easy to construct.

To build a 23 inch (58.4 cm) diameter, 24 inch

5-5

5-6
5-7

5–8 Ceramic fiber blanket kiln
Photo: the author

5–8

(61 cm) high kiln similar to the example pictured, the following materials are needed:

Two 27 inch × 8 foot (68.6 cm × 2.4 m) sections of expanded metal lathe
12 feet (3.7 m) of Insblanket, 1 inch (2.5 cm) thick
10 feet (3 m) of Kanthal wire
46 K-20 soft insulating bricks
3 K-20 hard firebrick soaps
One 15 × 15 inch (38 × 38 cm) silicon carbide kiln shelf

These materials are available from local ceramic suppliers or from the manufacturers listed on pages 97 and 98.

Stand one piece of metal lathe on edge and form it into a cylinder, slightly overlapping the ends. Cut short lengths of Kanthal wire with a wire cutter and tie the cylinder securely. To make the top of the kiln, place the cylinder upright on the second piece of lathe. Using the cylinder base as a pattern, cut the lathe with tin shears, leaving about an inch (2.5 cm) all around. Wire the top to the cylinder. Next, place the cylinder on top of the unrolled Insblanket. Using a felt pen, mark a circle slightly larger in diameter than the cylinder. Cut the blanket with scissors or a mat knife. Place the blanket circle inside the metal frame against the top. Bend 5 inch (12.7 cm) lengths of Kanthal wire into U-shapes. Push the ends of the wires through the blanket and frame, and twist the ends to secure the blanket to the frame.

To find the length of blanket needed for the kiln wall, lay the kiln frame on its side at the end of the unrolled Insblanket. Slowly roll the frame over the blanket one complete revolution. Allow a few extra inches (cms) for overlap, mark the position, and cut the blanket. Set the blanket snugly inside the frame and secure it with sufficient wire staples to prevent sagging. Cut a 2 × 2 inch (5 × 5 cm) hole in the top for a vent and two 2 × 2 inch (5 × 5 cm) spy holes on opposite sides, one high and one low. The damper and spy hole plugs are just scraps of Insblanket. The drum is now ready for use.

To construct the base of the kiln, first lay out a level foundation of packed earth or cement blocks. The example shown was built on a concrete slab. Make a floor of soft fire brick in a 27 inch (68.6 cm) square, using 6 parallel rows of 3 bricks each. On top of the floor, set one course of brick on edge in a smaller square, approximately 20 inches (51 cm) on a side, to form the walls of the firebox. Set the second course of brick directly on top of the first, lapping the joints. On one side of this course leave a half-brick opening for the burner port. Set the brick in the top course on the broad side to allow a wider base on which to put the drum. A brick placed diagonally at each corner with its ends cut at 45° angles will provide a tighter fit for the circular drum. Three hard firebrick soaps on end with a 15 × 15 inch

5-9 Raku kiln kit
Courtesy: Peach Valley Potters

5-10 Karen Wolf
Goddess
Earthenware; slab built, molded
5½ x 3¼ feet (1.7 x 1.0 m)

(38 × 38 cm) silicon carbide shelf on top form the floor of the ware chamber.

The burner, whether natural or liquid propane (LP) gas, should be placed at the port with a slight upward as well as sideward tilt to help create a circular flame pattern in the kiln.

A somewhat sturdier kiln can be constructed using 12½ gauge, 2 × 4 inch (5 × 10 cm) mesh, galvanized steel wire. Complete versions of this type of kiln are also commercially available.

The ceramic fiber blanket raku kiln has evolved to serve many functions. It can be used not only for firing unglazed and glazed pots, but for fuming and vapor glazing as well.

5-10

5-9

FUMING

To create lustrous, varicolored effects on a raku piece, the following method can be employed. After a piece has reached temperature, remove it from the kiln with tongs. Using an atomizer, spray a mixture of soluble salt, such as silver nitrate, and water on the hot glaze. Immediately return the piece to the kiln and reheat it to cone 018 (696°C/1285°F). Turn off the kiln and allow it to cool before removing the ware. In this manner, specific areas of a

5-11 M. Kauila Clark
Vase
Clay, slips; thrown, altered
8 x 3 inches (20.3 x 7.6 cm)

5-12 Rosemary Aiello
Container
Raku clay, slip; thrown, hand built
8 x 5 inches (20.3 x 12.7 cm)
Photo: Kathy Gardner

5-11

5-12

5-13 Harriet Brisson
Golden Eye
Raku clay, mirror plastic; slab built
7 x 7 feet (2.1 x 2.1 m)
Photo: W. R. Michael

5-14 Nancy April
Cloud Scape II
Raku clay; hand built
48 x 12 x 4 inches (122 x 30.1 x 10.2 cm)
Photo: Susan April

5-13

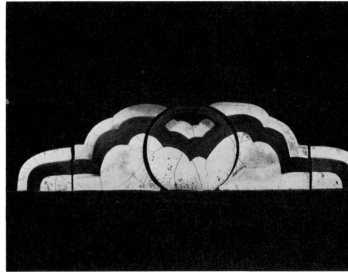

5-14

piece can be fumed and different salts can be used on a single piece. For safety, an approved vapor mask should be worn while spraying.

SALT-RAKU

Salt-raku, or soda vapor glazing, can be easily done in a blanket kiln. Only one change is necessary when the kiln is to be used for this purpose. When the brick is set up for the base, two half-brick openings should be left, one for the burner port and another in an adjacent side for a salting port. Two bricks on edge serve to close the salting port.

WARE

Usually the ware to be vapor fired is unglazed, either raw or bisqued. Slips or washes of colorant can be used for decoration. Thinly glazed pieces can also be vapor fired. Experimentation is necessary to discover which glazes will be enhanced by additional vapor glazing.

FIRING

The firing begins in the same way as a normal raku fire. When the ware has reached temperature, cut back the flame and fully open the top vent or damper. Open the salting port and throw a cupful of soda ash into the kiln. After a few moments, throw in more soda ash. Continue the process until the desired glaze surface is achieved. Turn off the kiln. Immediately remove the ware with tongs and place it in a bucket of combustible material for added smoke effects.

Additional information about soda vapor glazing and fuming will be found on pages 34–37 and 80–81.

A note on ceramic fiber refractories: Some people have complained of skin irritation when constructing or using kilns made of ceramic fiber refractories in blanket or bulk form. It is also possible for minute fiber particles to be inhaled. At present, testing is inconclusive regarding just how hazardous inhalation of these materials can be. In any case, it would be wise to use rubber gloves and a respirator mask when handling ceramic fiber refractories.

RAKU CLAY BODIES

Harriet Brisson's White

A.P. Green Fireclay	50
EPK Kaolin	15
Ball Clay	15
Grog	15
Talc	5

Tony Meccia's White

Pine Lake Fireclay	25
Cedar Heights Goldart	30
Ball Clay	15
Spodumene	5
Grog (fine)	15

Rick Berman's White

Fireclay	60
Ball Clay	30
Grog (55-mesh)	10

RAKU GLAZES

Tony Meccia's White

Gerstley Borate	50
China Clay	33
Flint	17

add 1 to 3% silver nitrate for gold luster

C/017 Clear Base

Frit 5301 (Ferro)	80
Borax	20
Bentonite	5

add:

Selenium (red in oxidation)	4
Copper Carbonate (turquoise in oxidation, copper luster in reduction)	5

Anne Hyland's C/06 White

Colemanite NA	47
Cornwall Stone	35
Barium Carbonate	12
Zircopax	6

David Davison's Simple White

Colemanite	80
Nepheline Syenite	20
Zircopax	12

Harriet Brisson's Crackle White

Gerstley Borate	40.5
Nepheline Syenite	33.8
Barium Carbonate	14.9
Flint	10.8

Chapter 6

VAPOR GLAZING

For centuries, salt has been used as a material for glazing ceramic ware. Traditionally, the process has been a high temperature single firing. When temperatures at or above cone 10 ($1285°C/2345°F$) are reached, common salt (NaCl, sodium chloride) is thrown into the kiln. The salt immediately volatilizes and the soda combines with the silica in the clay to form a hard, shiny glaze.

Over the past few years, clayworkers concerned with health, safety, and conservation have become wary of traditional salt glazing. One obvious problem is the ever increasing cost of the large amounts of fuel needed to reach the high temperatures. A more dangerous problem is that if a kiln is not properly salted, excess amounts of hydrochloric acid along with chlorine gas are released. Hydrochloric acid is hazardous to skin and plant life. Chlorine gas can damage lungs and ultimately cause death. To avoid these serious hazards, some people have begun to fire at lower temperatures and vapor glaze with materials other than salt. One such material, soda ash (sodium carbonate), seems particularly suited to vapor firing.

The chemical reaction of soda ash with clay is nearly identical to that of salt and clay. The difference is that no harmful byproducts are exhausted from the kiln.

Chemically, a series of reactions occur:

(1) $Na_2O \cdot CO_2 + H_2O \rightarrow 2NaOH + CO_2 \uparrow$
(2) $2NaOH + Q \text{ (heat)} \rightarrow Na_2O + H_2O \uparrow$
(3) $Na_2O + XAl_2O_3 \cdot XSiO_2 \rightarrow Na_2O \cdot XAl_2O_3 \cdot XSiO_2$

The soda ash reacts with the water vapor in the kiln atmosphere to form sodium hydroxide and carbon dioxide. The heat of the kiln decomposes the sodium hydroxide into sodium oxide and water vapor. The sodium oxide then reacts with the clay surface to form a sodium-alumina-silicate glaze. The carbon dioxide and water vapor exit from the kiln.

KILN

It is still a good idea to have a separate kiln lined with hard firebrick specifically for salt, or more properly, soda vapor firings. Soft brick will not stand up well to soda firing. During the firing, the soda reacts not only with the ware, but also with kiln shelves, posts, and interior walls. However, the vapors from soda ash do not attack brick as devastatingly as do salt vapors. Some clayworkers claim to notice very little such reaction and even alternate between normal reduction firings and soda vapor firings in the same kiln. In any case, to protect the kiln walls from rapid deterioration, coat them with aluminum oxide. Coat the silicon carbide kiln furniture with a wash of alumina hydrate before each firing. Kiln wash made of kaolin and flint should not be used because it will combine with the soda to become glaze, causing the pots to stick to the shelves. At low temperatures, the alumina hydrate wash is usually sufficient to prevent the ware from sticking to the shelves. For added safety, place three little balls, or *chits,* of clay rolled in flint under the foot of each piece as it is being set in the kiln.

Best glaze results occur in a downdraft kiln with salting ports located directly above the burner ports. Additional ports spaced in the kiln walls will help ensure good glaze coverage. Although the dangers of hydrochloric acid and chlorine gas are side-stepped when using soda ash, firings should still take place outdoors or in a very well-ventilated room. Soda ash gives off a somewhat acrid vapor which, if it escapes from the kiln in any way other than up the stack, can be irritating to the eyes, nose, and throat.

FIRING

A soda vapor firing proceeds like any other single fire process. Warm the kiln and then slowly bring up the temperature to cone 017 to 012 (727° to 876°C/1341° to 1609°F). Within that range, put the kiln into light to medium reduction to enhance the clay color. From then on, fire the kiln in reduction up to the temperature desired. Many clayworkers vapor glaze between cone 06 and cone 1 (991° to 1136°C/1816° to 2077°F). Because of the low melting point of soda ash, salting can begin as low as cone 012 (876°C/1609°F). Pyrometric cones will not react properly after the first salting because, like everything else in the kiln, they become glazed. Therefore, a pyrometer is recommended if accuracy is desired.

When stacking the kiln, place a few small rings of

6–1 Michael A. Chipperfield
Universal Gymnast #12
Three separate clay bodies, stains; extruded, thrown, slab built, assembled
13 x 14 x 11 inches (33 x 35 x 27.9 cm)

6–1

clay, or *draw trials,* near a spy hole. These will be used to indicate the amount of glaze being deposited on the ware as the salting progresses.

The method of introducing soda ash into the kiln depends on the surface desired on the fired ware. For an even coat of glaze, throw measured scoops of soda ash into each salting port. After ten minutes, hook out a draw trial with a long iron hook, cool it in water, and examine the glaze. Throw in more soda ash and pull another draw trial. Continue this procedure until a draw trial is pulled that is considered to have sufficient glaze. About two-thirds of a pound (300 g) of soda ash per cubic foot (.03 m³) of kiln space can be used initially until the amount of soda ash needed for an average firing is determined.

Warren Mather and Bernice Hillman introduce a mixture of soda ash and water into their kiln with a compressed air sprayer. In this manner, they use about one-half pound (227 g) of soda ash for a cone 01 (1117°C/2043°F) firing in their 25 cubic foot (.7 m³) kiln. By carefully spraying through many

6-2 Bernice Hillman
September 1978
Spodumene-talc clay, wood; slip cast
21 x 15 x 4 inches (53.3 x 38.1 x 10.2 cm)

6-2

cause the clay surface to become pitted. If ware has been coated with slips containing metallic coloring oxides, oxidation firing will prevent the vapor glaze from possible blistering.

SALT BISQUE

Paul Soldner emphasizes that his salt bisque ware is fired in a strongly oxidizing atmosphere. This helps bring out warm orange colors from unglazed fireclay pieces and soft pinks from porcelain.

STACKING

To obtain varicolored flash effects, tightly pack unglazed raw ware in a fuel kiln. Place magazines, brine-soaked rope, or other combustibles in and around the ware to help induce localized reduction. Strategically placed shards will protect parts of the ware from the salt vapor.

FIRING

Use very little salt in the firing. A handful in front of each burner before starting; another handful in each burner port around 800°C (1472°F); and once again at temperature, around 945°C (1733°F), is all the salt necessary to achieve pastel colorations.

DECORATION

Additional decoration can be made with white slip, or slips with 3 percent copper carbonate or .5 percent cobalt. Then coat the ware with a clear glaze and refire to the same temperature without salting. For smoke effects, remove the ware while it is still hot and place it in a container of combustible material.

different ports they achieve good coverage over all the ware.

If random vapor effects are desired, a mixture of soda ash and medium sawdust can be thrown into the ports at short intervals. David Davison uses about 5 pounds (2.3 kg) of soda ash mixed 60/40 with sawdust to vapor glaze in his 45 cubic foot (1.3 m³) kiln, getting flash effects and thin glaze coatings at cone 04 (1050°C/1922°F).

Vapor glazing can also be accomplished in oxidation firing. It is particularly effective if the clay used contains coarse iron particles. Reduction firing can

VAPOR GLAZE CLAY BODIES

David Crane's C/02 Vapor Firing Orange Clay Body

PBX Fireclay (30-mesh)	16.3
Pine Lake Fireclay (30-mesh)	13
Cedar Heights Goldart	16.3
XX Saggar (Tennessee)	16.3
Talc	8
Nepheline Syenite	3
F1 Wollastonite (fibrous)	4.1
Yellow Ochre	3
Grog (mixed mesh)	20

Bernice Hillman's C/1 Slip Casting White Clay

Kaolin (Pioneer)	30
Ball Clay	20
Talc	20
Spodumene	20
Flint	10

Dry Mix 20 pounds (9 kg)
Water   10 pounds (4.5 kg)
Sodium Silicate 3/8 oz. (42.5 g)

Chapter 7

EGYPTIAN PASTE

The earliest known glazes were probably discovered accidentally by Egyptians several thousand years ago. The paste material they used to model votive objects contained soluble sodium salts. When fired, these salts formed a thin, glassy coating on the objects. Two theories exist about these glazes, that they were formed from salts within the paste or from salts contained in the powder that the objects were packed in for firing. The latter theory has been successfully tested at Massachusetts Institute of Technology by Pamela Vandiver. In this process, the pieces to be glazed (usually beads or other small objects) are made from a thick paste of flint with small additions of calcium, feldspar, and gum binder. When the beads have completely dried, they are placed in a crucible partly filled with packing powder. This powder is a mixture of soda, potash, silica, calcium, and a bit of copper. The crucible is covered, placed in a kiln and heated to cone 09 (915°C/1679°F). When the kiln has cooled, the crucible is found to contain a solid lump of packing powder. The lump is easily crumbled to reveal the beads, completely glazed with a brilliant turquoise blue color. Further information on this method of producing self-glazed objects can be found in articles by Wulff et al., and Kiefer and Allibert (see Bibliography).

FORMING

The more commonly used method of forming self-glazing objects utilizes soluble salts directly in the body mixture. As an object is allowed to dry, these salts *wick out,* or rise to the surface, coating the entire object except where it rests on, or touches, another surface. When fired, the salts form a glaze.

7-1

7-1 Egyptian
Jar, 1558–1085 B.C.
4 x 3⅜ inches (10.1 x 8.6 cm)
Courtesy: Museum of Fine Arts, Boston

7-2 Egyptian
Canopic jars, 19th–20th Dynasty
Each jar approximately 12 x 6½ inches (30 x 16 cm)
Courtesy: Museum of Fine Arts, Boston

7-2

Because typical Egyptian paste bases contain little or no clay or other plastic materials, making objects of large size or volume is difficult. Work on the potter's wheel is virtually impossible without the addition of organic binders such as CMC or gum tragacanth. Even then it is difficult to make thin-walled vessels without resorting to excessive trimming. Further, trimming can prevent the soluble salts from forming a coating sufficient to provide a glassy surface when fired.

Slip casting will leach the salts into the plaster mold, so it, too, is an unsatisfactory way to form self-glazing objects.

Egyptian paste can, however, be used successfully for hand modeling and coil or slab building.

SLAB BUILDING

To make a flat slab, roll the paste between two cloths, using guide sticks for even thickness. Peel off the top cloth. Cut the slab to size and shape. Turn the slab onto a tightly stretched metal screen or window screen. Peel off the second cloth and allow the slab to stiffen. By allowing air to get at both the top and bottom of the slab, warping is minimized. If the slab is to be used as a tile, keep it on the screen until it is completely dry.

A slab object can be constructed in the usual manner using a watery slurry of the paste to help seal the seams. Handle the object as little as possible. Allow the finished piece to dry slowly. When dry, soluble salts will appear on all surfaces. Unwanted salts can be brushed from the bottom before the piece is placed in the kiln.

MOLDS

Objects may also be formed by pressing the paste into a mold. Molds can be made of plaster or from bisque fired clay. Press fairly stiff paste into the

7-3 Plaster press mold

7-4 Lawrence Conte
Scarabs, 1979
Egyptian paste; press molded
Largest: ⅜ x 1¼ x 1 inches (1.2 x 3.2 x 1.3 cm)

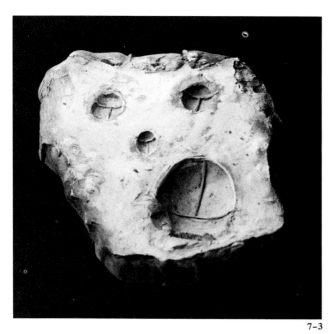

7-3

7-4

mold. Invert the mold and tap the paste object onto a piece of masonite, glass, or other nonporous surface. If the paste is left in the mold to set up, the salts will leach into the mold and no glaze will form when the piece is fired. Excessive handling after the object has been released from the mold can also create places where no glaze will form.

Egyptian paste can also be used over drape molds. Use the paste when it is fairly stiff. Remove the piece from the mold as soon as it is firm.

CORES

The ancient Egyptians often used fruit as a core over which to wrap and model paste slabs. Because the paste does not shrink, the fruit could be left inside until it was burned out during the firing. With this in mind, any organic or combustible object can be used as a core. A Styrofoam block, carved into an interesting form, can also be wrapped with slabs of

paste. Be sure there is a hole somewhere in the paste form to allow gases to escape from the burning core during the firing.

DIPPING

An easy way to make tiny beads is to dip string or straw into paste that has been thinned with water to a creamy consistency. Let the paste dry and then dip again. Repeat the process until the desired thickness is attained. Carefully break the dry paste into the lengths wanted, and fire. This method works best with a matt-surfaced paste or with the packing powder method of firing. Larger objects can also be formed in this manner. Crumpled newspaper, Styrofoam, and organic objects can be used as models for dip coating. An inflated balloon can be dip coated with paste. After the paste has become firm, deflate the balloon. All these cores will burn away when fired.

7-5 Nadia Farag Radwan
Scarab
Egyptian paste; carved
¾ x 1½ x 1 inch (1.9 x 3.1 x 2.5 cm)

7-6 Nadia Farag Radwan
Peasant Girl, 1978
White clay, Egyptian paste, underglaze, luster; cast, hand built
13 x 4½ x 3 inches (30 x 11.4 x 7.6 cm)

7-5
7-6

CARE IN HANDLING

Mix only enough paste to be used at one time or keep it in a tightly covered container. Otherwise, the paste will begin to dry and the soluble salts will start to disassociate from the paste. Work in progress should be covered tightly in plastic or lightly misted with water. Paste dries fairly quickly, but should be left uncovered and untouched for at least three days to allow the salts to fully bloom on the surface.

Because the paste is somewhat caustic, wash hands thoroughly when finished working.

COLOR

Aside from the turquoise blue color for which Egyptian paste is noted, a variety of other colors can also be produced. Two to 5 percent of copper carbonate added to a base paste will give the familiar turquoise. One to 2 percent of cobalt carbonate will give a rich blue. A 1 to 3 percent addition of manganese dioxide will give lavender to purple tones. Iron oxide in amounts from 6 to 10 percent will give brown or olive colors. Three to 5 percent of rutile will give tan. About 10 percent of almost any ceramic body stain added to a base paste will give a rich color. The firing temperature and materials used to make the base paste will influence these colors. Test samples are therefore recommended.

FIRING

Egyptian paste should be fired in an oxidation atmosphere. Large beads can be strung on lengths of Kanthal wire suspended between two firebricks. However, if the beads are too heavy or if too many

7-7 Bead tree

7-8 Star bead tree
Courtesy: Diamond Ceramics

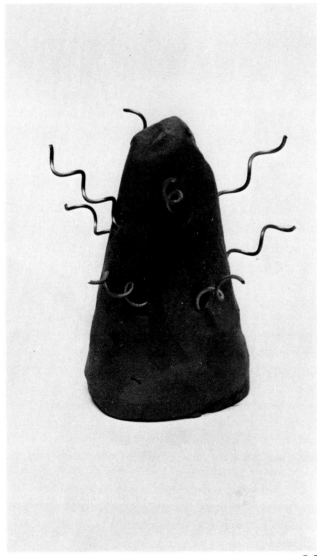

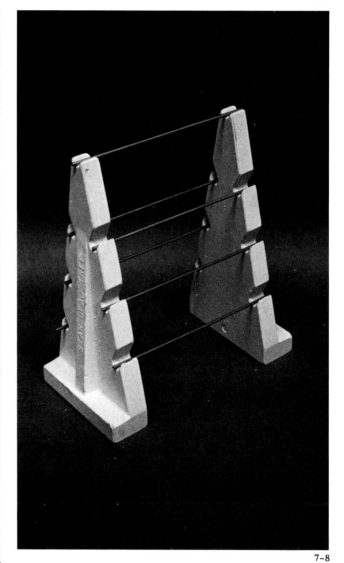

7-7

7-8

have been strung between the bricks, the wire will sag during the firing and the beads will fuse together. To prevent this, beads can be placed on a *bead tree,* a lump or cylinder of clay with short lengths of Kanthal wire stuck in it that has been bisque fired. Pieces of old kiln elements are well suited for this. Sturdy bead trees are now available commercially.

Other paste pieces can be placed on kiln shelves. To protect the shelves, coat them with a flint and kaolin kiln wash. After the wash has dried, dust on a coat of powdered whiting. This will prevent the paste from adhering to the shelves.

Fire the kiln slowly, especially if it contains solid objects. Accurate firing is important. If the kiln is

7-9 Nadia Farag Radwan
Mashrabia, 1979
White clay, Egyptian paste, underglaze, luster; slab built
16 x 22 x ½ inches (40.6 x 55.9 x 1.3 cm)

7-9

underfired, the result will be poor colors and a rough surface on the paste. Overfiring can cause the paste to bubble or melt.

EGYPTIAN PASTE BODIES

J. V. Noble's C/08 Gloss Paste

Soda Feldspar	46
Flint	23
Fine White Sand	9
Soda Ash	7
Soda Bicarbonate	7
Whiting	6
Bentonite	2

J. V. Noble's C/08 Matt Paste

Flint	56
Fine White Sand	22
Soda Ash	8
Soda Bicarbonate	8
Bentonite	6

C/04 White Egyptian Paste

Soda Feldspar	37.5
Kaolin	23.4
Flint	18.6
Soda Ash	5.7
Soda Bicarbonate	5.6
Ball Clay	4.6
Whiting	4.6

Chapter 8

EARTHENWARE

EARTHENWARE

Earthenware clays are the most abundant and therefore the easiest to obtain of all natural clays. When wet, earthenware clays appear in different colors from yellow, green, and blue, to sienna and black. After being fired from cone 08 to cone 02 (945° to 1101°C/1733° to 2014°F) the colors change to rich red oranges, browns, and deep blacks.

IMPURITIES

Working properties of these clays depend largely on which chemical impurities, granular substances, or organic materials they contain. As described in the chapter on choosing a clay, screening and washing will remove unwanted organic impurities and alkalies. Most early New England potters worked local clays with little refinement other than removing sticks and pebbles by hand before use.

The major impurity to be found in most earthenware clay is some form of iron compound such as magnetite (Fe_3O_4), hematite (Fe_2O_3), or pyrite (FeS_2). While the iron content gives earthenware its characteristic rich color, it is also its chief limitation. Clays containing a large percentage of iron oxide (FeO) will not fire to vitrification. The iron forms compounds with other materials in the clay which fuse and melt around cone 5 (1177°C/ 2151°F). Reduction atmospheres can cause melting

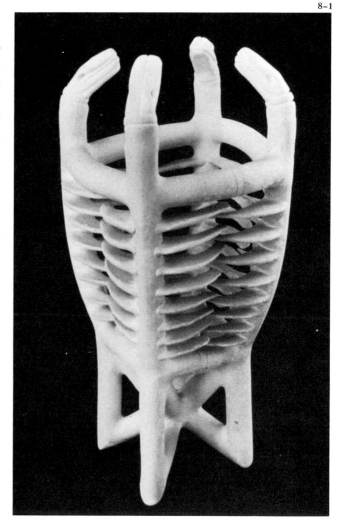

8-1 Dean Smith
Container for Air, 1977
White earthenware; hollow tube construction
20 x 13 x 10 inches (50.8 x 33 x 25.4 cm)

8-2 Christopher Gustin
Jar, 1977
Terra cotta, slip; thrown, altered
13 x 11 inches (33 x 27.9 cm)

8-2

8-3 Roman
Vase, 1st century B.C.
2⅞ x 3⅜ inches (7.3 x 8.7 cm)
Courtesy: Museum of Fine Arts, Boston
  Bequest of Charles Hoyt

8-4 Richard J. Barrett
Rare Bird
Earthenware, underglaze
17 x 42 x 5 inches (43.2 x 106.7 x
  12.7 cm)

8-5 Author
Bank of Happiness, 1976
Earthenware, luster; slab built
15 x 7 x 20 inches (38.1 x 17.8 x 50.8 cm)
Private collection

8-3

8-6
8-7

8-4
8-5

8-6 Zuñi Pueblo
Canteen
Earthenware, slip; coil built, burnished
Height: 12 inches (30.1 cm)
Courtesy: National Museum of Natural
   History, Smithsonian Institution

8-7 Jalisco, Mexico
Canala water pot
Earthenware, slip
Height: 15 inches (33.1 cm)
Photo: Jens Art Morrison

8-8 Bernard Palissy
Oval Dish, late 16th century
Earthenware, polychrome glaze;
   molded, hand modeled
22 x 17½ inches (55.9 x 44.5 cm)
Courtesy: Museum of Fine Arts, Boston
   Arthur Mason Knapp Fund

8-8

8-9 Tom Supensky
Cup in Its Proper Perspective V, wall piece, 1978
Earthenware, underglaze, luster; thrown, altered
Diameter: 14 inches (35.6 cm)

8-9

8-10 Grueby Faïence Company
Bulbous Vase, c. 1900
Earthenware; molded, hand modeled
12⁵⁄₁₆ x 3⅛ inches (31.7 x 7.8 cm)
Courtesy: Museum of Fine Arts, Boston
  Anonymous gift in memory of John Pierce

8-11 Turker Ozdogan
Balkan Gypsy
Terra cotta; thrown, hand modeled
Height: 40 inches (101.6 cm)
Photo: Robert Wayne Randolph

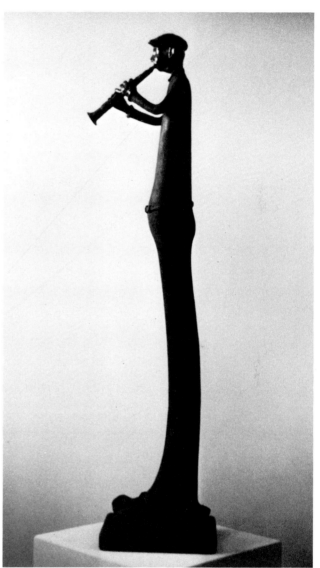

8-10

8-11

to begin as low as cone 02 (1101°C/2014°F). If the clay contains pyrite, bloating can occur as well.

Efflorescence, or scumming, on the surface of fired earthenware can occur because the calcium sulfate ($CaSO_4$), present in most clays, does not begin to decompose until far hotter temperatures have been reached. Small amounts of barium carbonate ($BaCO_3$) added to the clay will prevent scumming. The barium combines with the sulfate to form barium sulfate ($BaSO_4$). This compound, used in X-ray diagnosis, is insoluble and nontoxic.

8-12 Peter Gerbic
Table
Earthenware; slab, coil built
22 x 30 x 30 inches (55.9 x 76.2 x
   76.2 cm)

8-13 Mary Ann Davis
Japanese country–style stove
Earthenware, metal grill; coil built
24 x 18 inches (61 x 45.7 cm)

8-14 Graham Marks
Coil construction
Earthenware; coil built
25 x 28 inches (63.5 x 71.1 cm)
Collection: Mr. and Mrs. Ira Epstein
Photo: Jerry Schmidt

8-12
8-13

8-14

FORMING

A plastic earthenware clay will lend itself well to all forming methods. Earthenware bodies can also be compounded for slip casting.

DECORATION

Earthenware clay will work well with almost any decorating technique. Early New England decorating techniques consisted largely of brushed-on oxide washes or slip trailing.

GLAZE

Historically, most earthenware was coated with simple lead-silica glazes which became glossy when fired. This helped to make the ware waterproof,

8-15 Roman
Brick
Terra-cotta; molded, stamped
3⅛ x 5⅞ x 1⅝ inches (8 x 14.6 x 4 cm)
Courtesy: Museum of Fine Arts, Boston
  Gift of C. Grenville Way

8-16 Mexican scove kiln
Photo: Bruce Wood

8-17 Firing scove kiln
Photo: Bruce Wood

but imparted a slight yellowish cast to the clay color. Today, with the dangers of lead well known, other glaze materials are preferable. Nonlead frit or gerstley borate glazes will give excellent clear gloss results without danger of lead release.

FIRING

For the warmest colors, earthenware should be fired either in saggars or in a strongly oxidizing atmosphere. In some cases, mild reduction will bring about deeper browns and blacks. Strong reduction can cause pieces to bloat, slump, or melt.

The ware should be fired slowly and evenly up to temperature to prevent cracks or explosions. Because of the lower firing range, few glazes fuse with the clay as is the case with higher temperature clay and glaze. A soaking period at maturity, however, will help ensure a good bond between earthenware and glaze.

BRICK

Brick has been used in construction since ancient times. Examples of fired brick have been dated as

8-15

8-16

8-17

far back as 600 B.C. in Babylonia. By the first century, Romans were using brick extensively for buildings and roadways.

Usually, brick is made from local clay. It is fashioned into rectangular forms for ease in constructing walls. Brick sizes may vary according to the place

8-18 Babylonian
Detail of Royal Processional Street,
  c. 651 to 604 B.C.
Earthenware; carved, glazed
35¼ x 90¼ inches (89.5 x 229.2 cm)
Courtesy: Museum of Fine Arts, Boston
  Marie Antoinette Evans Fund

8-19 Mexican brickmaker
Photo: Bruce Wood

8-20 George T. Mason
Hands, 1976
Terra cotta tile; carved
4½ x 4½ feet (1.4 x 1.4 m)

8-18
8-19

of manufacture or because of a particular use. In 1679, a Massachusetts Bay Colony court ordered that all earthenware brick be made 9 X 2¼ X 4½ inches (22.9 X 5.7 X 11.4 cm) in size. Today, in the United States, although common brick has been standardized at 8 X 2¾ X 3¾ inches (20.3 X 8 X 9.5 cm), there is still variation. Brick from a single company will often be different with each firing.

In many countries, brick is fired in scove kilns which are built of dried brick and fired from within. When the kiln has cooled, it is dismantled and its bricks are used for building.

ORNAMENTAL BRICK

While brick itself is a plain building material, it can be used in much more ornamental ways. The Royal Processional Street in Babylon (c. 651 to 604 B.C.) is a fine example of the use of brick as a highly decorative architectural element.

8–21 Nino Caruso
Interior, Evangelic Church, Savona,
 Italy, 1967
White earthenware tile; slip cast
Tile size: 11 x 5 x 1 inches (28 x 13
 x 2 cm)

8–22 Jim Stephenson
Brown X
Brick clay; press molded
24 x 24 x 1½ inches (61 x 61 x 3.8 cm)
Photo: David Shelly

8–23 Nino Caruso
Wall, Galerie Les Champs, Paris, 1968
White earthenware brick; extruded
 (positive/negative)
Brick size: 12 x 8 x 6 inches (30 x 20 x
 15 cm)

8–20
8–21

8–22
8–23

8-24 Author
Style, 1975
Earthenware flue pipe; carved
32 x 9 x 9 inches (81.1 x 22.9 x 22.9 cm)

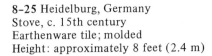

8-25 Heidelburg, Germany
Stove, c. 15th century
Earthenware tile; molded
Height: approximately 8 feet (2.4 m)

8-24

8-25

Wall reliefs can be carved from leather hard common brick obtained from a local manufacturer. If raw brick is not available, individual units can be made in simple, rectangular wooden molds.

MOLD

Place the wooden mold on the ground or other flat surface. Tamp stiff clay into the mold and then slide the mold up and away from the clay. Dry each brick evenly by placing it on different sides as it hardens. It is difficult to control the density of individual bricks with this method, and they may vary considerably in size when fired. If a large quantity of similar brick is required, a hand-operated press is commercially available.

The CINVA-Ram Block Press was originally designed for use in underdeveloped countries to aid

8-26 Bernard J. Felch
Wall detail
Manganese brick; carved
Portion of wall: 5 x 32 feet (1.5 x 9.8 m)
Courtesy: Bank of Delaware, Wilmington
Photo: David McClintock

8-26

8-27 Clayton Bailey
Robot Teapot
White clay; slip cast
3 x 6 x 10 inches (20.3 x 15.2 x
    25.4 cm)
Photo: Dr. Gladstone

8-28 Nancy Selvin
"Paper" Teapot
White clay; underglaze; slab built from
    cast pieces
8½ x 5 x 5 inches (21.6 x 12.7 x
    12.7 cm)

8-29 David Middlebrook
Dig In, 1976
White clay,
40 x 20 x 30 inches (101.6 x 50.8 x 76.2 cm)

8-30 Donna Nicholas
Coal Kite
Stoneware clay; extruded, slab built
26 x 24 x 18 inches (66 x 61 x 45.7 cm)

in making building blocks from common earth. Because it is simple to operate, has the capacity to make flat floor tile or blocks as large as 11½ X 5½ X 3½ inches (9 X 14 X 29 cm), and can make hollowed block forms, it is ideal for making brick for decorative use as well.

If a carved brick relief is to be integrated into a wall made of standard brick, be sure to take the clay shrinkage into account. Make the mold large enough so that the brick will be the proper size when fired.

Press molding or slip casting brick and tile can offer a wide range of finished forms. By varying the arrangement of simple press molded forms, some clayworkers can compose a virtually endless array of interesting images. Other artists have their designs commercially slip cast or ram-pressed to produce thousands of tiles to use in large architectural installations.

WHITEWARE

Whiteware does not refer to a geological clay classification, but to a type of finished ware. Historically, whitewares were the outcome of efforts by European clayworkers to imitate the porcelains imported from the Orient. The emphasis was on a creamy surface, delicate design, and translucent ware. Even today, most commercial producers of whiteware still emphasize these qualities. Studio artists appear more interested in low fire white clay bodies primarily for their color. A white body acts as a background which heightens the color of low fire stains and glazes.

To gain whiteness in a low fire clay body, talc and other nonclay materials are added. Therefore, a talc body is usually less plastic than stoneware. This inconvenience is offset by the relative ease of clay mixing and the less expensive cost for materials.

Although the reduced plasticity may make large thrown forms more difficult to execute, hand-building techniques are not adversely affected. In fact, with some talc bodies, objects may be made with thick walls or even modeled solidly. When fired slowly, these pieces will not crack or explode, as is often the case with other clays. Because they are less plastic, whiteware bodies are also well suited for

8-27
8-28

8-31 Martha A. Holt
My Studio Floor on Saturday, 1978
Talc clay, wood; press molded, slip
cast
48 x 36 x 24 inches (122 x 91.4 x
61 cm)
Courtesy: Theo Portnoy Gallery

8-32 Anne M. Cembalest
Red Cabbage
Earthenware, acrylic paint; hand built
14 x 14 inches (35.6 x 35.6 cm)
Photo: John Wapner

8-33 Peter Shire
Cosmos Baseball Teapot, 1977
White clay, copper tube; thrown, coil,
slab, extruded
15 x 7¼ x 24 inches (38.1 x 18.4 x
61 cm)
Photo: Jack Freed

8-29

8-30

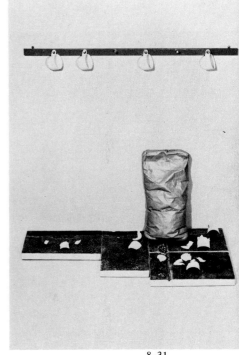

8-31

8-32

8-33

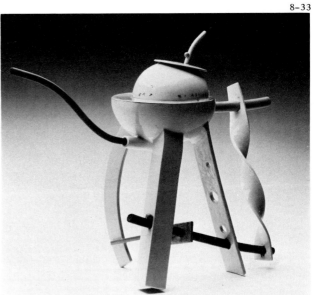

8-34 Victor Spinski
Kentucky Fried Chicken and Beer, 1978
White clay, photo decals, luster; slip cast, slab built
10 x 15 x 15 inches (25.4 x 38.1 x 38.1 cm)

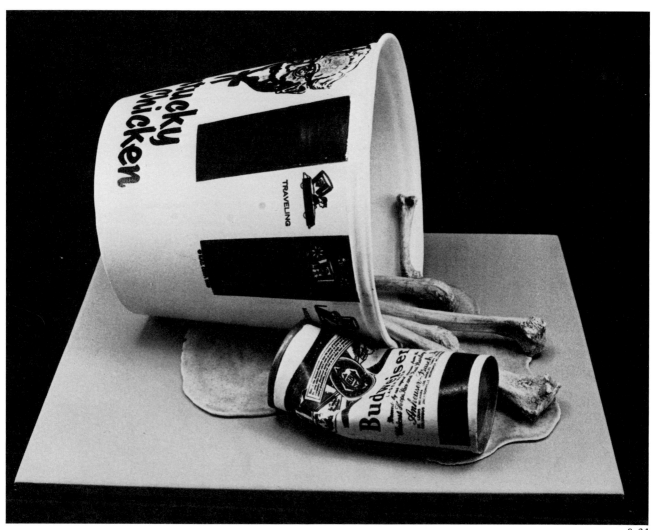

8-34

slip casting. Often, only a small amount of deflocculant such as soda ash need be added.

Commercial low fire white clay bodies for hand building and casting are readily available.

GLAZE

The overwhelming number of commercial glazes available within broad color and texture ranges make it unnecessary to formulate other than the most basic cover glaze in the studio.

DECORATION

Techniques that work well with whiteware, such as underglaze, china painting, decals, and photoclay, will be discussed in subsequent chapters.

8-35 Patricia Lay
Untitled, 1975
Clay, commercial tile, metal, glass, wood, luster; slab built
1 x 7 x 9 feet (.3 x 2.1 x 2.7 m)

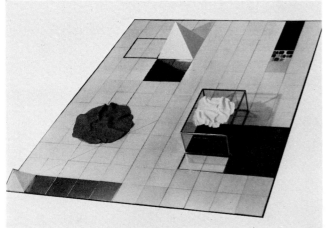

8-35

FIRING

The brightest colors are obtained through firing in an oxidation atmosphere. While whiteware will not suffer as greatly as earthenware when fired in reduction, it will lose its clear whiteness.

LOW FIRE CLAY BODIES

David Middlebrook's C/04 White

Ball Clay	50
Fireclay	50

Red Earthenware C/04

Cedar Heights Redart	71.4
Ball Clay	10.7
Flint	10.7
Feldspar	7.2

Helaine Ettinger's C/04 Terra Cotta

Cedar Heights Redart	60
Cedar Heights Goldart	15
Pine Lake Fireclay (30-mesh)	15
Talc	10
Barium Carbonate	0.75

White Talc Body C/06-04

Talc	50
Ball Clay	40
Nepheline Syenite	10

White Casting Slip C/04

Talc	45
Ball Clay	19
Kaolin	17
Feldspar	19
+ .15% Sodium Silicate	
.15% Soda Ash	

John Frantz' C/03-1 Red Clay

Cedar Heights Redart	35
Fireclay	30
Ball Clay	25
Talc	10

CONE 04 GLAZES

Christopher Gustin's White

Frit 3124 (Ferro)	40
Gerstley Borate	30
Nepheline Syenite	25
Flint	5
+ Zircopax	8

Semi-matt

Frit 3191 (Ferro) or K-3 (Hommel)	34
Lithium Carbonate	3
Zinc Oxide	23
Kaolin	20
Flint	20

John Frantz's Clear Gloss

Gerstley Borate	30
Kaolin	25
Frit 3124 (Ferro)	30
Flint	15

Soft White Matt

Frit 3134 (Ferro)	44
Kaolin	12
Dolomite	8
Whiting	8
Flint	28

John Frantz's White Slip

Ball Clay	35
Kaolin (Grolleg)	15
Frit 3124 (Ferro)	10
Flint	20
Gerstley Borate	5
Talc	5
	90
+ Tin Oxide	5
or Zircopax	10

Chapter 9

NONFIRED FINISHES

Effects that vary from the subtle to the garish can be produced by using nonfired coatings on ceramic objects.

Rub oils, waxes, or shoe polish into porous fired clay to give warm, soft colorations.

PAINTS

Use oil, acrylic, or enamel paints for bright colors or to alter surface textures. Water soluble dyes and paints can also be used, but cover them with fixative, clear varnish, or acrylic to preserve the colors.

STAINS

Commercial nonfiring ceramic stains are available as opaques, translucents, pearls, and metallics. To apply nonfired stain, brush, pour, spray, or sponge it onto dust- and oil-free bisque fired ware. Be sure to work the stain well into the surface, and wipe off any excess before it dries. When dry, the stain will withstand normal cleaning with water.

To completely color a clay surface, apply opaque stain. For shading or antique effects, apply translucents or metallics on top of a dry opaque and immediately wipe off any excess. The use of a sealer is recommended between applications and as a finish coat.

TEXTURES

Glitter or flocking can impart very different appearances to a ceramic object. First, coat the fired clay with white glue. Sprinkle the material onto the wet glue. When the glue has dried, tap or blow off the excess material. It is important that the glue be applied evenly and that a generous amount of material be spread over it. Although additional glitter can be glued on without much trouble, a poor application of flocking is difficult to patch.

Chapter 10

TERRA SIGILLATA

Terra sigillata originally referred to certain Roman pressed or embossed ware (*terra,* earth; *sigil,* seal, stamp). Later, the term came to denote Greek and Roman earthenware that had been decorated with an unglazed, shiny surface. This coating was a refined clay slip.

MAKING TERRA SIGILLATA

To make terra sigillata, choose a low firing red clay, such as Cedar Heights Redart, Osage, or other fine-grained earthenware. Fine-grained high temperature

10-1

10-2

clays can also be used with varying results. To a liter of water (distilled, if possible), add 1 cc of a defloc-culant such as soda ash or Calgon and mix well. Add 500 g of clay and let it slake for about fifteen minutes. Shake or stir the mixture vigorously and then let it settle for at least twenty-four hours. Pour off everything, except the heaviest material, into another container. Discard the heavy material. Remix the saved portion and allow it to settle for

10–1 Graeco-Roman
Cup, 1st century B.C.
Earthenware; press molded
2½ 3⅜ inches (6.5 x 8.6 cm)
Courtesy: Museum of Fine Arts, Boston
  Gift of Henry P. Kidder

10–2 Attic
Stamnos, c. 450 B.C.
Earthenware, terra sigillata; coil, press
  molded, burnished
10½ x 11¼ inches (26.7 x 28.6 cm)
Courtesy: Worcester Art Museum,
  Massachusetts. Bequest of Mrs.
  Charlotte E. W. Buffington

10–3 Christine Federighi
Medicine Chest
Talc clay, terra sigillata; slab, hand built
16 x 12 x 5 inches (40.6 x 30.1 x
  12.7 cm)
Photo: Susan Kurtz

10–3

10-4 Kurt Wild
Blackware pot
Earthenware, terra sigillata; hand built, burnished
4½ x 6 inches (11.4 x 15.2 cm)
Collection: Dr. Edward A. and Carol Brown
Photo: Jens Gunelson

10-4

another twenty-four hours. Pour off the top two-thirds of the mixture into a flat pan and allow it to dry by evaporation. The drying time can be hastened by putting the pan on top of a stove or hot plate and boiling off the water. The resulting terra sigillata should be ground with a mortar and pestle and then passed through an 80-mesh or finer sieve.

APPLICATION

Mix a 50-50 batch of terra sigillata powder and water to make a creamy slip. Brush or spray this on leather hard ware. For a harder, glossier finish, polish the coated surface with a soft cloth as soon as it is dry and then burnish with a smooth rock or spoon. A few drops of cooking oil can be used to lubricate the spoon while burnishing.

FIRING

To keep the shiny surface and color of ware coated with terra sigillata, fire to cone 06 (991°C/1816°F) or lower. Higher firing can dull the surface.

COLOR

Most natural terra sigillata will fire from red to brown in oxidation and black in reduction. Other colors can be made by mixing 3 to 10 percent of colorant, such as copper, cobalt, manganese, or ceramic body stain, with 30 percent dry terra sigillata and 70 percent water.

REDUCTION DECORATION

For a matt decoration on a polished surface to be reduction fired, use a mixture of 50 percent fire clay and 50 percent ball clay in water. Better results can be obtained by applying the following mixture:

Ball Clay	45.8
Bentonite	17.3
Frit (Pemco 25, Ferro 3819, or Hommell 259)	16.5
Talc	13.4
Nepheline Syenite	6.4
Calgon	.6

Add water and mix to a creamy consistency.

Even though properly fired terra sigillata may give the appearance of a shiny glaze, the ware itself will not usually be waterproof.

Chapter 11

UNDERGLAZE

Decorations made with underglaze are quite durable because they are fired under a protective glaze. However, because underglazes must stand up to the maturing temperature of the cover glaze, the color palette is somewhat limited.

PIGMENTS

Underglaze pigments can be formulated in the studio by dry mixing up to 30 percent stain or raw oxide colorant with 65 percent or more feldspar or frit and 5 to 10 percent clay. Grind this mixture well on a glass slab with a 50-50 blend of pine oil and balsam. A ratio of 60 oil to 40 pigment is a recommended starting point. Thin as needed with a few drops of turpentine.

Commercial underglaze is available in a variety of ready-mixed colors. It may be purchased in liquid form in jars, semimoist in pans, in tubes, or as crayons and pencils. Most commercial underglazes will retain their colors up to cone 1 (1136°C/2077°F). Some blues and greens will fire as high as cone 6 (1201°C/2194°F) without changing color.

11-1

11-1 Patti Warashina
Moth Ball
White clay, underglaze, china paint; slab, cast, hand built
28 x 18 x 14 inches (71.1 x 45.7 x 35.6 cm)

11-2 Marvin Bjurlin
Hinged Double Form (closed and open)
Talc clay, wood, metal, underglaze; slab built
9 x 4 x 28 inches (22.9 x 10.2 x 71.1 cm)
Photo: Judy Durick

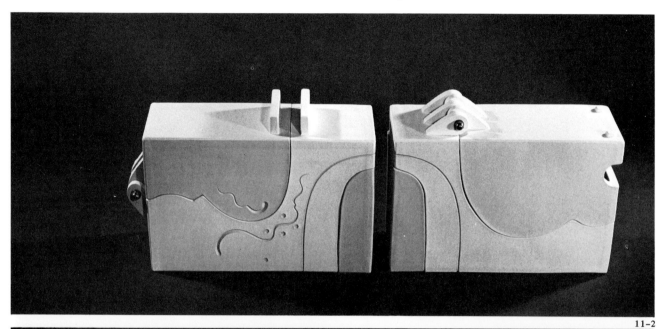

11-2

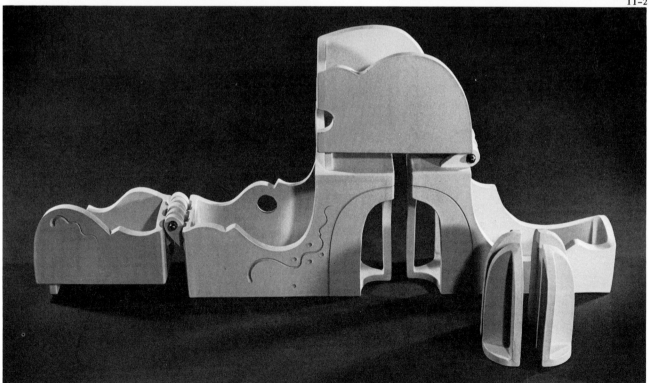

11-3 Beryl Solla
Carrot Plate
Talc clay, underglaze, luster; thrown
Diameter: 14 inches (35.6 cm)

11–4 Bill Suworoff
Untitled (Ostrich with Power Pack), 1978
White clay, underglaze; molded, hand built
71 x 21 x 37 inches (180.3 x 53.3 x 94 cm)
Courtesy: Fendrick Gallery

11–4

11-5 Anna Salibello
Plate, 1979
Talc body, underglaze; thrown, altered
Diameter: 20 inches (50.8 cm)

11-6 Karen Thuesen Massaro
Iron with Parakeet, 1977
White clay, underglaze; slip cast
9 x 10 x 4½ inches (22.9 x 25.4 x 11.4 cm)
Photo: Linda Young

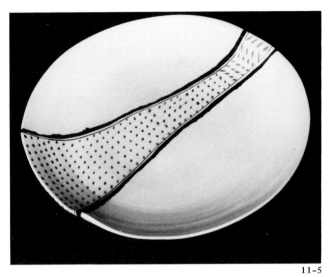

11-5

11-6

APPLICATION

Underglaze decorations can be applied to raw or bisqued ware by brushing or spraying. They can also be stamped on with foam rubber or rubber stamps. Decorations can be directly printed by silkscreen or copperplate methods or printed on decal sheets and applied as transfer prints.

INTERMEDIATE FIRE

Before being glazed, oil-based underglaze decorations must go through a *burning-off* or *hardening-on* fire. This intermediate fire is usually taken to cone 017 (727°C/1341°F) to decompose oils, burn off carbon, and fuse the pigment to the clay body. Because most commercial underglaze is water based, the hardening-on fire can be eliminated. However, if the cover glaze is to be brushed on, a hardening-on fire is recommended to prevent the decoration from being accidentally smudged.

Another way to eliminate the necessity of a hardening-on fire is to apply the underglaze to raw ware which is then bisque fired before the cover glaze is applied.

The absorption rate of the fired underglaze should be the same as the clay body so that the cover glaze will be uniform and not pit or blister. To help prevent the cover glaze from crawling, do not heavily apply the underglaze.

COVER GLAZE

Colors can be affected by the cover glaze. High alkaline and calcium glazes will tend to enhance many underglaze colors. Lead-based glazes, while heightening the brilliance of some colors, will adversely affect cobalt blues and chrome greens. Zinc and magnesium will alter chrome-based colors. Glazes high in barium or boron can affect red and pink underglazes.

To avoid distorting an underglaze decoration, a suitable cover glaze should be clear and have little fluidity when fired.

11-7 Elizabeth Leitner
Enclosed Canyon
Earthenware, underglaze, polyester resin; slab, hand built
1 x 5½ x 3 feet (.3 x 1.7 x .9 m)
Photo: David Graham

11-7

FIRING

The glaze firing should reach maturity fairly quickly. Prolonged firing can cause colors to fade and make the cover glaze flow. It is important that the firing be strongly oxidizing, otherwise the colors will be severely altered.

Chapter 12

MAJOLICA

Brightly decorated Spanish pottery shipped to Italy in the ninth century was known as Majolica. Renaissance Italian polychrome ceramics were called Faïence by the French. The British referred to decorated tin-glazed Dutch ware as Delft. All these names identify an in-glaze technique of ceramic decoration.

Although historical examples of this technique have been traced back as far as the fifth century in Mesopotamia, the term Majolica specifically designates ceramic ware of the type produced in Italy during the fifteenth century. This ware was generally a hard-bisqued red earthenware coated with an opaque lead-tin glaze. After the ground coat had dried, decorations of cobalt, copper, iron, and other stains were brushed on. The ware was then fired to the maturing temperature of the glaze, usually around cone 010 (887°C/1629°F). The technique as practiced required a high level of skill. An error in brush stroke could deposit too much stain or rub off the ground coat. Attempts at repairs would become indelibly obvious after firing.

Slight variations in the materials and a little practice make it possible to obtain spectacular results with fewer problems.

12-1

GROUND COAT

Any reliable glaze, preferably a gloss or semigloss with little fluidity, can be used as a ground coat. For best results, the glaze should be opacified with tin oxide, but zirconium compounds make acceptable substitutes. When mixing the opaque ground coat,

12-1 Mexican
Covered jar, c. 1977
Earthenware; thrown
Height: 8 inches (20.3 cm)
Photo: Jens Art Morrison

12-2 Attributed to Giovanni Maria
Inkstand, c. 1500
Earthenware; slab built
3½ x 7⅞ x 11 inches (8.9 x 20 x 27.9 cm)
Courtesy: Museum of Fine Arts, Boston
  J. H. and E. A. Payne Fund

12-2

add a gum such as CMC to improve the dry strength of the glaze. The harder the ground coat, the less likely it is to be accidentally rubbed off. A coat of gum applied over the dry ground coat will also help prevent smudging.

Another way to have a hard-surfaced ground coat is to add a small amount of acrylic medium to the water that is to be mixed with the glaze. About 5 cc of medium to every 100 cc of water will usually make the applied glaze dry quite hard. Mix only enough glaze to be used in a short time. As the acrylic medium sets, the glaze becomes too stiff to properly apply.

To get an even surface, the ground coat is best applied by dipping or spraying. Dipping results in a smooth surface which helps preserve intricate decorations. Spraying puts an even layer of tiny bumps on the glaze surface. These will slightly diffuse the decoration when fired, causing a softer appearance.

Either greenware or bisque may be decorated in this manner – provided the appropriate ground coat is used.

COLORANTS

Colorants can be either oxides and carbonates or ceramic underglaze stains. Overglaze stains are not effective because they often change color or burn out when the ground coat is fired to maturity. The colorants may be mixed directly with water in a very thin solution. If the solution is too thick, the decoration will fire quite dark, possibly metallic black. For softer colors, mix equal parts of colorant and the ground coat base with water. Adding 1 or 2 percent of acrylic medium will help the decoration to dry hard and prevent smudging.

12–3 Lambeth Delft
Adam and Eve, 1680 to 1700
Earthenware; molded
Diameter: 16½ inches (41.9 cm)
Courtesy: Museum of Fine Arts, Boston
  Gift of G. E. Hawes

12–3

12-4 Emmett Leader
Teapot
Earthenware; slab built
7 x 5 x 8 inches (17.8 x 12.7 x 20.3 cm)

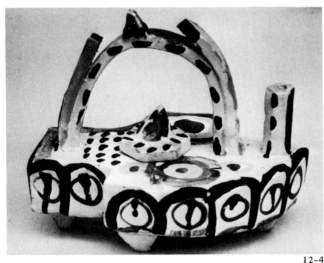

12-4

APPLICATION

Apply the decoration by brush or airbrush with a quick, firm hand. If acrylic medium has been used to harden the ground coat, decorations can be laid out in advance, using a soft 4B pencil. Hesitations show up as darker splotches when fired. Attempts at repairing errors usually are very obvious after the ware has been fired, so careful planning is important.

It is often easier and wiser to remove all the glaze and start over than to attempt repairs. If acrylic medium is used, heat the ware above 350°C (662°F) to burn off the medium. When the ware has cooled, wash off the glaze. To remove the glaze without heating the ware, scrape it off with a single-edged razor blade.

While Majolica ware is most often decorated by hand brushing, different effects may be achieved by using sponge stamps or airbrushed stencils.

Majolica is generally fired in saggars or in an oxidation atmosphere for bright colors. The technique can work as well when fired in reduction, provided the proper base glaze and colorant proportions are used.

MAJOLICA GLAZES

Emmett Leader's White Base C/04 (from V. Cushing)

Nepheline Syenite	20
Gerstley Borate	30
Frit 3195 (Ferro)	30
EPK Kaolin	10
Flint	10
+ Bentonite	2
+ Plastic Vitrox (or Cornwall Stone)	15

Helaine Ettinger's White Base C/04–03

Frit 3124 (Ferro)	44
Frit 3304 (Ferro)	35
EPK Kaolin	3
Kona F-4 Soda Feldspar	3
Zircopax	4
Tin Oxide	11
+ Bentonite	2

Chapter 13

CHINA PAINTING

China painting, or overglazing, is a method of applying bright colors to a fired glaze surface. Historically, china painting was often confined to decorating blanks of commercially glazed bone china vessels or tiles. Today, china paints are no longer merely embellishment; they are usually integrated into the design of a particular ceramic object.

China paints are mixtures of colorants, stains, clays, and fluxes which have been fired in a frit furnace, ground into fine powder, and prepared for use. A facsimile of china paint can be made by adding from 1 to 10 percent glaze stain to a mixture of 85 percent lead or alkaline frit and 15 percent ball or china clay. Before using, this mixture should be thoroughly ground in a dry ball mill or with a mortar and pestle. The resulting powder should pass through a sieve that is at least 150-mesh.

PREPARATION

To prepare china paint for application, tap a bit of the powder from its container onto a clean glass slab. Add about one-half that amount of binder oil such as copaiba balsam, aniseed oil, or CMC gum. Add a few drops of turpentine to soften the mixture while grinding it with a palette knife. Dip a quill brush or other fine brush into the bottle of turpentine, stroking off the excess on the bottle lip. Then draw the brush through the mixed paint and check the consistency on a test palette. If the paint dries too quickly, add a few drops of oil. If it stays shiny too long, add a bit more powder and regrind the paint.

MOIST PAINTS

A number of ceramic color companies now offer a wide variety of china paints semimoist in tubes or ready-mixed in jars. Although these paints can be used directly from their containers, it is still a good idea to grind them with a palette knife on a glass slab to ensure proper consistency. It may also be necessary to thin the paint with the manufacturer's recommended thinner or with a few drops of turpentine.

APPLICATION

Using alcohol, throughly clean the object to be decorated and allow it to dry. Apply the paint very thinly so that it looks clean and somewhat transparent.

After decorating the piece, dry it completely before firing. Air drying could take 10 to 12 hours. The paint can be slowly dried in a warm oven set at

13-1 Niderviller, France
Plate, 18th century
Earthenware, china paint; molded
Diameter: 7½ inches (19 cm)
Courtesy: Museum of Fine Arts, Boston

13-1

115°C (239°F) with the door ajar. If the paint is dried too fast, it might curl and flake off.

Protect the ware from dust while the paint is being applied and while it is drying. Dust spots can mar the finished design.

All excess paint should be cleaned off before the ware is fired. If the paint is still wet, it can be cleaned off with a brush dipped in turpentine. For precise cleaning, allow the paint to dry and then scratch off the unwanted paint with a mat knife or a single-edged razor blade. Clean around the decorated area with a cloth dipped in alcohol to get rid of any specks of paint or fingerprints. Brushes should be cleaned in turpentine first and then alcohol. If the paint on the glass slab should dry, it can be reused by adding a few drops of turpentine and then grinding it.

China paints can also be applied by using silk-screen techniques.

LINES

A soft 4B pencil or india ink, both of which burn off when fired, can be used to lay out a design on

13-2 Diana Harmon Jackson
Clock, 1978
White clay, mechanism, china paint; hand built
8 x 22 inches (20.3 x 55.9 cm)
Photo: Bernie Hitzig

13-2

clean, dry ware. Should there be an error when applying the paint, the india ink has the advantage of not washing off with water or turpentine.

If the outline is to be a permanent part of the fired design, prepare a mixture of 5 parts paint and 1 part confectioners' sugar. Grind this together with a few drops of water and apply with a fine brush or pen. When the drawing dries, it will be resistant to turpentine, but can be removed with water. When fired, the sugar burns away and the paint becomes permanent.

13-3 Charles Malin
May, 1956, 1978
White clay, china paint; slab built
30 x 22 x 4 inches (76.2 x 55.9 x 10.2 cm)

LARGE AREAS

Filling in large areas of color by brush can leave undesired streaks. One way to lay a ground, or evenly coat a glazed surface, is to pad the china paint on with a small piece of foam rubber.

Mix one part color with half as much binder oil and a tiny amount of flux such as a low-melting frit. Grind this well, then add a few more drops of oil and spread the mixture over the surface with a wide brush or a spatula. Then, folding the foam rubber over a finger, gently pad the entire area to even out the color. The more the paint is padded, the lighter the color becomes. When finished, protect the surface from dust and allow the paint to dry before firing. Discard the foam after use.

Another way to lay a ground is by using dry powdered paint. Coat the parts of the object not to be colored with a solution of sugar water and dye. When the sugar has dried, brush on a mixture of linseed oil and turpentine. Pad this mixture with a piece of foam rubber to eliminate brush marks. Immediately dust powdered paint onto the oil with soft cotton and then blow off the excess. After the piece has dried for twenty-four hours, wash it with water to remove the sugar. Dry the piece and then fire it.

An airbrush can also be used to fill in large areas of color. Mix the paint, grind it thoroughly, and thin it with commercial thinner or acetone. A few drops of silkscreen medium can be added to facilitate drying. The usual precautions for spraying (properly vented spray booth, vapor mask) are in order. Clean the airbrush with alcohol immediately after use.

Protect areas not to be painted with masking tape or sugar solution. Remove the tape after the paint has dried.

FIRING

Most china paints can be fired in oxidation to cone 014 (834°C/1533°F). Certain reds will burn out if they are fired higher than cone 016 (764°C/1407°F). Some blues and purples must be fired to cone 013 (869°C/1596°F) or they will retain a matt surface. Special fluxes listed by the manufacturers can be added in small amounts to lower the maturing temperatures of these colors.

China paints, with the exception of certain blacks, can be fired several times. If a complicated decoration is desired, it is often better to do it in stages with firings in between. In many cases, a second application of the same paint is needed to bring out the best color.

13-3

Chapter 14

LUSTER GLAZE

FUMING

Fuming is a method of creating iridescent films or lusters on the surface of a fired glaze. These films are brought about by introducing certain metallic salts into a kiln during the cooling stages of a firing. Fuming can be done on ware that has been fired in soda vapor kilns, in fuel fired kilns, or in electric kilns.

A traditional way of fuming utilizes cast iron pots filled with salts strategically placed among the ware in a kiln. When the iron pots heat sufficiently, the salts volatilize and coat nearby glazes. This method requires ports in the kiln walls large enough to accommodate the iron pots.

For a less hazardous technique of fuming, use a length of angle iron or a long handled wrought iron spoon. Load the spoon, or the V of the angle iron, with salts. Put the iron through a spy hole and tap it vigorously. As the salts are shaken off the iron, they volatilize almost immediately and spread throughout the kiln.

A long, steel tube can also be used for fuming. Fill one end of the tube with salts. Insert the tube into the kiln through a spy hole and direct it at a particular piece. Blow hard through the tube. The salts will spray out, volatilize, and coat the ware.

In each technique, fuming is done during the cooling stage of the firing when the kiln is at cone 018 (696°C/1285°F). As soon as the salts have been introduced, the kiln should be sealed to prevent escape of any fumes. Because it is difficult to maintain the same temperature overall, large kilns do not usually lend themselves to even fuming. This, however, is not necessarily a disadvantage. Sometimes the effects caused by uneven fuming are more interesting than even applications. If even fuming is desired, additional ports are needed throughout the entire kiln.

SAGGAR FUMING

By using a saggar, a few objects can be fumed while other pieces in the kiln remain untouched. This method is particularly effective when using an electric kiln. Not only is other ware protected from the fumes, but the kiln elements are protected as well. Place the pieces to be fumed in a saggar along with a fired clay bowl filled with a mixture of soda ash and coloring oxide. Cover the saggar and put it in the kiln. During the firing, the soda ash/oxide mixture volatilizes and covers the ware with a thin glaze coating. To protect the interior of the saggar, give the walls a thin wash of alumina hydrate before each use.

GLAZE

High iron glazes and those with low acid and low lime will take on the most interesting fumed effects. Soda vapor glaze also accepts fuming very well.

14-1 Persian
Bowl, early 13th century
Earthenware, luster; thrown
4 x 8¹⁵⁄₁₆ inches (10.2 x 22.5 cm)
Courtesy: Museum of Fine Arts, Boston
  Gift of Goelet Foundation

14-2 Deruta, Italy
Vase with cover, 1530 to 1540
Earthenware, luster; thrown, molded
14⅝ x 11⅝ inches (36.7 x 29.3 cm)
Courtesy: Museum of Fine Arts, Boston

14-1
14-2

SALTS

The salt which consistently gives extraordinary and varied iridescence is stannous chloride. Bismuth nitrate will also give pearly lusters. Cobalt nitrate yields blue colors. Cupric chloride effects green to red shades. Lustrous yellows can be achieved with silver chloride or silver nitrate. Chromium nitrate goes from greens and yellows to shades of red. These metallic salts can be used alone or in combination to give varied and unexpected color effects.

The use of zinc oxide is an exception to the typical process of fuming while the kiln cools. If finely powdered zinc oxide is introduced into the kiln at the finishing temperature of the firing, high iron clays will take on a yellow green to green glazed surface.

For safety, an approved vapor mask should be worn when doing any fuming. Proper kiln ventilation is also important.

LUSTER GLAZE

Luster glazes are thin, reflecting, metallic overlays fired onto the surface of a glaze. Historically, luster glazes were achieved by applying metallic salts to glaze fired ware. The ware was then refired in a kiln that was strongly reduced toward the end of the firing. Using this method, mixtures of red or yellow ochre, gum, and soluble salts such as copper sulphate, bismuth subnitrate, silver nitrate, or gold chloride can result in iridescent colors like red, purple, yellow, or ivory. Copper and silver carbonate can also be used with varying results.

NATURAL LUSTERS

To make a luster mixture, add about 25 percent by weight of a colorant to ochre. Mix this with gum or fat oil (thickened turpentine) and grind it to a smooth consistency. Brush or spray a thin coat of the mixture onto gloss glazed ware and allow it to dry completely. Fire the ware in oxidation to the temperature at which the glaze just starts to melt. While holding that temperature, reduce the kiln heavily for at least a half hour. Keep the kiln in reduction while it is cooling down. This may be done either by keeping a low flame in the kiln with the damper almost closed or by introducing combustible materials to maintain a smoky atmosphere.

An alternate method of holding reduction in the cooling stage is akin to the secondary reduction process in raku. After the work has been soaked in reduction for a half hour, turn off the kiln. Remove the ware with tongs and immediately place it in a pit lined with combustible material. Cover the pieces with earth and leave them to cool. After the ware is uncovered, it may need to be washed to remove dirt and carbon film. If so, use a cloth and warm soapy water. Anything more abrasive might rub off the luster.

RESINATE LUSTERS

Luster resinate glazes should be prepared in a well-ventilated area. Wear rubber gloves, an apron, and eye protection. The procedure is a simple one; resin is melted and a metallic salt is stirred in.

To prepare a clear pearlescent luster, the following materials are needed: 30 parts by weight powdered pine resin (available at chemical supply houses), 10 parts bismuth nitrate and 75 parts lavender oil. In a glass container, slowly melt the pine resin over a hot plate. When the resin liquefies, raise the temperature slightly. Add small portions of the bismuth while stirring vigorously. When the color changes to brown, slowly stir in the lavender oil. Allow the mixture to settle and cool. Filter or decant the liquid and the glaze is ready to apply. Store the resinate in a dark place.

More complete information on formulating res-

inates can be found in works by Parmelee and by Shaw (see Bibliography).

COMMERCIAL LUSTERS

Today the luster glazes most widely used by clayworkers are ready-to-use commercial preparations. They are easily available, generally of consistent quality, require no special preparation, and come in a wide variety of colors. Because these lusters consist of minute particles suspended in a medium, they should not be shaken. Any residue that settles to the bottom of a container should be discarded.

To thicken a luster glaze, simply leave the cover off the container for a time. To thin a luster, use the thinner recommended by the manufacturer, adding only a few drops at a time with an eyedropper.

Because most lusters have the color and consistency of maple syrup as they come from the container, it is wise to make sample palettes of all the glazes to be used. Fire separate palettes to the upper and lower temperatures recommended by the manufacturer. In this way, the color variations for each luster when used over a particular base glaze can be discovered. A one cone difference in temperature can make a pink luster fire blue.

APPLICATION

Lusters can be applied by pouring, brushing, airbrushing, and sponging. Luster glaze should be applied to dust-free, clean, dry, gloss glazed ware. Use acetone or denatured alcohol to clean off dust, grease, skin oils, and glaze residues. If the ware is not well cleaned, the luster will not adhere properly.

Glazes should be applied in a thin, even coat. A heavy application will cause the glaze to run. After the ware has been decorated, it should be thoroughly dried in a dust-free area.

Brushes In order to avoid contamination of the

14–3 Susan G. Stephenson
Trojan Soup Tureen
High fired porcelain, luster; thrown, altered
7 x 14 inches (17.8 x 35.6 cm)

14–3

lusters, cleanliness is important. Because the fine glaze particles are difficult to totally remove, a separate brush should be used for each luster. Clean the brushes immediately after each use with the luster manufacturer's recommended cleaner or denatured alcohol. Because the alcohol contains water, be sure the brushes are completely dry before their next use.

For best results, a variety of good quality brushes are helpful. Camel hair *cut liners* in different sizes are best for banding. Large *square shaders* will give relatively even fill over large areas. Short *spotters* or

14-4 Victor Spinski
Trash Can, 1976
Talc clay, decals, photo decals, luster; slip cast, hand built
24 x 18 inches (61 x 45.7 cm)

painters can be used to fill small areas. Badger, fitch, or glass *stipplers* can be used to give mottled effects. In all cases, natural hair or bristle brushes are recommended because synthetic materials will not carry the luster glaze well.

Airbrush If an airbrush is used, it, too, should be thoroughly cleaned immediately after each use, or else the needle and tip will clog. Occasionally an air brush will spit during use because of a buildup of glaze on the tip. If this happens, clean the needle and tip with a cotton swab dipped in cleaner or denatured alcohol. Again, allow the airbrush to dry completely before continuing. Water will cause white spots or spots of base glaze to show through the luster after it has been fired.

When airbrushing lusters, use a well-ventilated spraybooth and wear a vapor mask. Many luster glazes contain toluene, chloroform, and other potentially harmful substances.

Sponging Applying luster glaze with a sponge can give interesting mottled effects. Cut off a portion of a natural sponge, dip it in slightly thickened luster and daub it onto the glazed surface. Discard the piece of sponge after use.

FIRING

Luster glazed ware must be fired in an oxidation atmosphere. Lack of sufficient oxygen can cause a clouded appearance, discoloration, and poor abrasion resistance. Although a fuel fired muffle kiln can be used, best results can be obtained by using an electric kiln. The kiln should be adequately vented to the outdoors.

Stack ware loosely throughout the kiln, with at least 2 inches (5.1 cm) of space between the ware and the shelves above. This will allow even heating and adequate ventilation. Crowding the ware can

14-4

cause glaze vapors from one piece to adversely affect another.

The firing should proceed slowly to about 450°C (842°F) with the kiln door ajar and the spy holes open. This will ensure that all carbon and organic matter have burned away. Close the door and slowly fire the kiln to the desired temperature. Too rapid a firing might cause the ware to split because of thermal shock. By keeping the spy holes open throughout the fire, a good oxidation atmosphere

14–5 Author
Mirror, 1977
High fired stoneware, mirror, luster; slab, hand built
19 x 12 x 1 inch (48.1 x 30.1 x 2.5 cm)
Private collection

14–6 Author
Kupboard, 1977
High fired porcelain, luster, wood, brass, acrylite; hand built
Each cup: 4 x 2 inches (10.2 x 5.1 cm)
Collection: J. Patrick Lannan

will be ensured. When temperature is reached, a short soaking period will allow the lusters to bond completely with the base glaze. Then turn off the kiln and close the spy holes. Allow the kiln to become cold before it is opened for unstacking.

Most luster glazes mature between cone 020 and cone 018 (625° to 696°C/1157° to 1285°F), but some can be fired as high as cone 010 (881°C/1629°F) without adverse effects. When firing lusters onto low fire glazes, the lower maturing temperatures are usually sufficient to bond the glazes together. Underfired lusters or lusters applied too thickly will powder off after firing. Overfired luster colors tend to burn out.

14-6

14-5

SPECIAL EFFECTS

For greater brilliance and depth of color, additional coatings of the same luster can be applied and fired after each application.

When using two or more lusters on a piece, each one may need a different temperature for its best color. Be sure to apply and fire first the glaze that requires the highest temperature so that it will not be lost in subsequent firings.

Overlays Because of the basic formulas of lusters, it is not possible to mix them together in the way that pigments might be mixed. However, multiple firings using different color overlays can create fascinating color effects. Gold, palladium, or platinum, in particular, can be applied and fired as the undercoat. Then, if a transparent color is applied and fired at a slightly lower temperature, varicolored effects can occur.

Different colored luster glazes may be applied one over another while still wet, creating interesting but unpredictable streaked effects.

14-7 Author
Covered jar, 1975
High fired stoneware, luster; thrown
6 x 6 inches (15.2 x 15.2 cm)
Private collection

14-7

Novelty Glazes Some manufacturers have preparations to bring about halo, weeping, or marbleized effects. These should not be overlooked as methods for obtaining striking glaze effects, particularly when used in conjunction with the usual application techniques.

Matt Lusters All the luster glazing techniques mentioned so far are recommended for use over hard gloss glazes. Many of the colored luster glazes will have softened, more subdued effects if fired on matt or semimatt glazes. Gold and other metallic lusters, however, will tend to look muddy if fired on nongloss glazes.

Errors or unwanted fired luster glaze can be removed by careful rubbing with a gold eraser. If the entire application appears unsatisfactory, refiring to midrange temperatures will burn out all the luster glaze so that the piece can be completely relustered.

If metallic lusters should tarnish, they can be buffed lightly with a silver polishing cloth. Anything more abrasive might scratch the glaze.

Chapter 15

DECALS

Decals, decalcomania, or on-glaze lithographs have been in use by the ceramics industry for over two hundred years as a means of replicating specific decorations. A typical decal is made by copperplate engraving, lithographing, or silkscreening an over-glaze image in reverse onto a gelatin coated paper. This transfer paper is then placed face down on a freshly varnished glazed surface and rubbed to secure the print. After the varnish has dried, the paper is washed off with water, the ware is dried and then fired.

WATERMOUNT DECALS

Watermount decals, more commonly available to the clayworker today, have the image printed right side up on simplex paper which has been coated with a soluble material. The image is then coated with lacquer and dried. To use a watermount decal, cut the chosen image from its mounting sheet. Place it in room temperature water or between the folds of a dampened towel long enough for the paper to become thoroughly wet. Slide the decal face up from its backing onto a glazed surface that has been cleaned with acetone. Starting from the center and working outward, use a stiff piece of cardboard or rubber squeegee to force all water and air from under the decal. Blot surface water with a dry cloth.

If the decal is not adhered carefully, the image may fire improperly.

UNDERGLAZE DECALS

Underglaze decals, often used by industry, usually require a bonding agent or an intermediate firing to harden on the decal and burn off residues before final glazing. For these reasons, few studio clay-workers use this type of decal. However, Commercial Decal Inc. does produce custom nonhardening-on, watermount underglaze decals in minimum orders of 500.

STUDIO-MADE DECALS

More and more people are choosing to make their own decals using silkscreen or photosilkscreen techniques. This offers a virtually infinite variety of images, without having to rely only on those that are commercially available. Images requiring more than one color need a separate screen made, or cut, for each color. When printing more than one color, proper alignment, or registration, is essential. If a screen of 130-mesh is to be used, be sure that the glaze materials are at least 140-mesh or finer so that

15-1 Chinese
Export plate, *Autumn* (after Cipriani), c. 1785
High fired porcelain, decal; molded, pierced
Diameter: 11½ inches (29.2 cm)
Courtesy: Museum of Fine Arts, Boston
 Gift of the Winfield Foundation

15-1

15-2 Eric L. Blecher
Indirect Object
Talc clay, photo decal; slab built
6 x 18 x 20 inches (15.2 x 45.7 x 50.8 cm)

15-3 Nancy Selvin
Wall piece
White clay, underglaze, decals; slip cast
13 x 15 inches (33 x 38.1 cm)
Photo: Steve Selvin

15-2

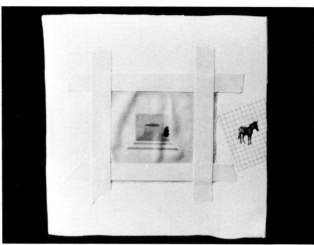

15-3

they pass smoothly through the screen without damaging it. Water-based ceramic pigments do not coat or cover as well as those that are in an oil base. Add the glaze pigments to a mixture of equal parts Damar varnish, boiled linseed oil, and turpentine until a creamy consistency is reached. Commercial silkscreen medium can also be used in a ratio of 60 medium to 40 glaze pigment. Screen the image onto either commercial decal paper or paper that has been prepared with a thin coat of starch. When the first color has dried, align and screen the second color. Repeat the process until all the colors have been screened onto the paper. After everything is completely dry, apply a thin coat of varnish or clear acrylic paint to the entire paper. Upon drying, the pigments will be bonded to this top coating. Then cut the decal and apply it to a glazed surface in the same manner as a regular watermount decal.

If particularly intricate or accurately colored decals are desired, it is often best to have them commercially made. A number of decal companies will make custom ceramic decals, some of which are listed on pages 97–98. Most companies have a minimum order per design.

FIRING

Dry decaled ware thoroughly before firing. It is important that the kiln be fully oxidizing throughout the fire, particularly in the early stages when organic and carbon compounds are vaporizing off the decals. An electric kiln is therefore recommended. Keeping the spy holes open during the entire firing will help ensure good oxidation. The firing should proceed slowly with a steady temperature climb. When using commercial decals, fire to the manufacturer's suggested temperature to obtain the best results. However, interesting results can sometimes be obtained by overfiring. Some colors may burn out, but others may alter with unexpected effects. The firing temperature for studio-made decals will depend upon which raw materials have been used to make the decal.

Underfired decals may powder or flake off. To correct this, accurately align another copy of the decal directly over the flawed one, allow it to dry and then refire to the proper temperature. In most

15-4 Michael Duvall
Tea set
High fired porcelain, stain, decal, luster; thrown, slab, extruded
Tray: 1½ x 9½ x 12½ inches (3.8 x 24.1 x 31.8 cm)

15-4

cases, this will repair the error. If not, start all over again on another piece.

Placing decals on top of fired luster glaze is not recommended because decal residues can combine with and discolor the luster. Because most decals can be fired somewhat higher than luster glaze, it is often better to apply and fire the decal first. Then apply luster glaze and fire to a slightly lower temperature.

Chapter 16

PHOTOCLAY

Photosensitizing ceramics, or photoclay, is a method of decorating a ceramic form that can give unique and intriguing results. It is a complex process which requires an understanding of darkroom photography techniques and ceramic techniques. The basic process consists of coating a glaze fired surface with a light-sensitive material. A photographic image is developed on the material and then permanently fixed to the glaze by being fired in a kiln.

The photographic image to be reproduced may be in the form of either a prepared positive transparency or a regular black-and-white photo negative.

POSITIVE TRANSPARENCY

There are a number of ways to produce a positive transparency. The easiest one is to have a commercial printer prepare the transparency from a particular print or negative.

In a darkroom, one way to make a positive transparency is by exposing a black-and-white negative onto Contrast Process Film (CPF). Although a good slide projector is adequate for projecting the image, a photographic enlarger will give more accurate results. Focus the negative on an enlarging easel or board to the size of the desired print. Close the lens to its smallest aperture and expose the image at 2 second intervals on a test strip of CPF. While a typical exposure might be 10 seconds at f/16, a particular negative might require a different time. Wearing rubber gloves and a rubber or plastic apron, develop the film in Kodak DK50 for 4 minutes, fix, wash, and let the film dry thoroughly before using.

Positive transparencies are a good way to accurately reproduce repeated images on multiple production pieces.

CONTACT PRINTING METHOD

Contact printing from a positive transparency onto ceramic ware should be done in a well-ventilated darkroom under yellow safelight. Clean a piece of glaze fired ware with acetone or household bleach. Brush or spray a coating of Kodak Photo Resist emulsion (KPR) onto the ware. Dry this either in a warm oven or in front of a low speed fan. Apply a second coating of KPR and dry it thoroughly.

If a brush is used to apply the KPR, apply the first coat horizontally and the second coat vertically, or vice versa. This will fill in any gaps in the application and help prevent streaking.

After the sensitized surface is dry, carefully position the transparency face-up on the ware. To assure close contact between the transparency and the

16-1 Martha A. Holt
China Clay Polaroids, 1977
White clay, underglaze, KPR emulsion, china paint, Plexiglas;
  slip cast 17 x 13 x 2 inches (43.2 x 33 x 5.1 cm)

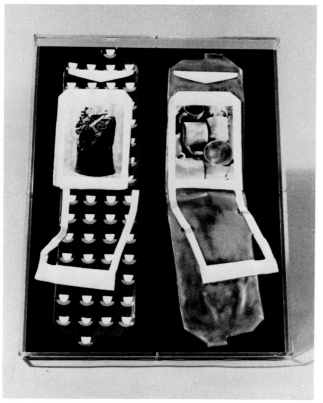

16-1

DEVELOPING

The developer used for KPR is n-butyl acetate. Wearing gloves and an apron, mix a chosen commercial china paint or overglaze with normal n-butyl acetate to a creamy consistency. Brush this mixture over the KPR. The image develops instantaneously. Allow the surface to dry and then lightly sponge off any excess pigment under running water. Use acetone to clean off unwanted emulsion. Then dry the ware completely. If the ware has absorbed any water from the photochemicals and is fired before completely dry, small patches of clay may blow off. This unfortunately common defect, called *spitting-out,* can be avoided by slowly warming the ware before firing. Fire the ware to the recommended overglaze temperature.

PROJECTED TRANSPARENCY METHOD

A positive transparency can also be used to put an image on a curved surface by projection. Under red safelight conditions, brush or spray a thin coating of Kodak Ortho Resist emulsion (KOR) on a clean, glazed surface. Because KOR is oxygen sensitive, keep it in an airtight container and use only small amounts at any one time. Use a warm oven to dry the ware. Do not use a fan.

Use a tungsten light projector or photo enlarger to project the image onto the sensitized surface. Put a red filter over the projector, project and focus the image. Remove the filter before exposing the KOR. Make test strips, using glazed clay, to determine the best time for a particular transparency. A typical exposure might be 4 minutes at 12 inches (30.1 cm) with a 500 watt bulb.

KPR surface, place a sheet of glass on top of the transparency. However, if the surface is slightly irregular, do not use glass. Instead, tape down the edges of the transparency and set small weights on the opaque parts of the image. It is essential that the transparency have full contact with the KPR surface, otherwise the image may come out blurred or uneven.

Once the transparency is in place, use a sunlamp to expose the image. A typical exposure with a 275 watt sunlamp is about 8 minutes at 12 inches (30.1 cm). Making a test strip of glazed, fired clay with 2 minute exposure intervals beforehand, will help determine the best exposure for a particular transparency.

DEVELOPING

Brush or pour a creamy mixture of n-butyl acetate and overglaze color over the exposed surface. Allow the ware to dry and then sponge off the excess pigment under running water. KOR emulsion remains soft, so care should be taken to prevent accidental scratches. Unwanted emulsion can be cleaned away with acetone. Be sure the ware is completely dry before firing to the recommended overglaze temperature.

PROJECTED NEGATIVE METHOD

Photosensitizing a glazed ceramic surface in this way eliminates the need for preparing a positive transparency. A regular black-and-white photo negative is projected directly onto the sensitized surface. This method is particularly effective if one-of-a-kind images are desired for a group of serial ceramic pieces.

PREPARING PHOTOEMULSION

The necessary photoemulsion is prepared under red safelight conditions. Wear rubber gloves and a rubber or plastic apron. In a glass container, dissolve 10 g of gelatin in 360 cc of warm distilled water. Add 32 g of potassium bromide and .8 g of potassium iodide. Stir to dissolve. Heat the mixture to 55°C (131°F) and hold at that temperature.

Dissolve 40 g of silver nitrate in 400 cc of distilled water. Stir this into the potassium bromide solution while maintaining the temperature. Add 40 g of gelatin to set the solution. Allow this to cool for three to four hours. When the emulsion has jelled, shred it through cheesecloth into 3 liters of room temperature distilled water. Allow this to stand for three minutes, then pour off the water. Repeat the process three more times to wash away any soluble salts. Wash the remaining emulsion under running water for fifteen minutes and drain. Refrigerate the emulsion in a light-tight container until needed.

PRINTING

Under a red safelight, slowly heat the emulsion in a stainless steel container on a hotplate to 55°C (131°F). Allow it to cool to 40°C (104°F) and then hold at that temperature. Apply the emulsion evenly over a prewarmed, glazed surface by brushing, pouring, or spraying. Dry the ware completely in a warm oven or in front of a small fan. Use a test strip of glazed clay to find the best time for the negative in use. A typical exposure might be f/8 for 20 seconds at 12 inches (30.1 cm).

With a red filter on the enlarger, project the negative onto the ware to find focus and position. Shut off the enlarger and remove the filter. Expose the sensitized surface for the required length of time. Develop the image in Dektol for about 2 minutes, fix, and wash in cool water for about 10 minutes. Remove unwanted emulsion with household bleach. Dry the ware thoroughly, prewarm, and then fire to cone 013 (869°C/1596°F).

PICCERAMIC

Kits to produce photoclay decorations are available through the Picceramic Company. If the manufacturer's directions are carefully followed, this patented process can be used to produce remarkably clear, dense images on glaze fired ware. The standard kit contains all the emulsion and chemicals necessary to produce up to 25 images of dinner plate size. Larger kits and separate chemicals are also available.

16–2 Author
Beth, 1976
High fired stoneware, Picceramic process; slab built
14 x 8 x 2 inches (35.6 x 20.3 x 5.1 cm)

16–3 Author
Beth, 1976
High fired stoneware, Picceramic process; slab built
16 x 7 x 4 inches (40.6 x 17.8 x 10.2 cm)

16–2

16–3

COLOR

The color of the fired image, generally red brown, can vary depending upon the raw materials used to formulate the base glaze on the ware. Chemical color changes have been suggested by the manufacturer. Instead of using the last solution included in the kit, the following substitutions can be tried: To a solution of 1000 cc of distilled water and 10 cc of 98 percent hydrochloric acid, add 10 g of:

ferric or manganous sulphate for a blue-white image

cobaltous sulphate for a grey-green image
nickel sulphate for a yellow-green image
stannous sulphate for a white image
uranium sulphate for a reddish image
vanadyl sulphate for a yellow image

Picceramic has recently introduced its *Direct Positive Photoceram* emulsion. It is used to make monocolor images on ceramic objects by direct projection of positive color transparencies, eliminating the need for an internegative.

The Picceramic images should be fired to cone 014 to 013 (834 to 869°C/1533 to 1596°F). Temperatures as low as cone 017 (727°C/1341°F) have also been effective, depending on the base glaze used.

When stored out of direct sunlight, the processing chemicals mixed as stock solutions have a shelf life of one year. Unmixed chemicals are stable for three years. The shelf life of Photoceram emulsion is one year if refrigerated, or more than eight years if stored in a freezer.

At present, multicolored images can be produced only by separate firings of single color overprints or through hand tinting with transparent lusters or china paints.

BASE GLAZE

For the clearest image, use the preceding photoclay methods on hard, gloss glaze. A transparent gloss on white clay, or a white gloss on dark clay, will give the best resolution to a photoclay image. Interesting and unusual effects may be obtained if the image is produced on top of matt glazed surfaces or colored glazes.

Bibliography

A Guide to Overglaze Decoration for the Ceramist. East Newark, New Jersey: Hanovia Liquid Gold, 1976.

Boudreau, Eugene H. *Making the Adobe Brick.* Berkeley, California: Fifth St. Press, 1971.

Brisson, Harriet. "Sawdust Firing," *Ceramics Monthly,* vol. 24, no. 8 (October, 1976), pp. 39–41.

Jorgensen, Gunhild. *The Technique of China Painting.* New York: Van Nostrand Reinhold Company, 1974.

Kaplan, Jonathan. "Making Ceramic Decals," *Ceramics Monthly,* vol. 23, nos. 4 and 5 (April, 1975; May, 1975), pp. 18–21; 40–44.

Kiefer, Charles and Allibert, A. "Pharonic Blue Ceramics, The Process of Self-glazing," *Archaeology,* vol. 24, no. 1 (April, 1971), pp. 107–117.

Kingery, W. D. *Introduction to Ceramics.* New York: John Wiley and Sons Inc., 1960.

Lawrence, W. G. *Ceramic Science for the Potter.* Philadelphia: Chilton Book Company, 1972.

Naked Clay. New York: Museum of the American Indian, 1972.

Nigrosh, Leon I. *Claywork: Form and Idea in Ceramic Design.* Worcester, Massachusetts: Davis Publications, Inc., 1975.

Noble, Joseph Veach. "The Technique of Egyptian Faïence," *American Journal of Archaeology,* vol. 73, no. 4 (October, 1969), pp. 435–439.

Norton, F. H. *Ceramics for the Artist Potter.* Reading, Massachusetts: Addison-Wesley Publishing Company, 1956.

_____. *Elements of Ceramics.* Second edition. Reading, Massachusetts: Addison-Wesley Publishing Company, 1974.

Parmelee, Cullen W. *Ceramic Glazes.* Third edition. Revised by Cameron G. Harman. Boston: Cahners Books, 1973.

Riegger, Hal. *Primitive Pottery.* New York: Van Nostrand Reinhold Company, 1972.

Schindler, F. E. "Decorating Glass with Lusters," Reprint from *The Glass Industry.* East Newark, New Jersey: Hanovia Liquid Gold, 1966.

Shaw, Kenneth. *Ceramic Colors and Pottery Decoration.* New York: Frederick A. Praeger, Inc., 1969.

Troy, Jack. *Salt Glazed Ceramics.* New York: Watson-Guptill Publications, 1977.

Tyler, Christopher and Hirsch, Richard. *Raku.* New York: Watson-Guptill Publications, 1975.

Watkins, Lura Woodside. *Early New England Potters and Their Wares.* Cambridge, Massachusetts: Harvard University Press, 1950.

Williams, Gerry. "Photoresist," *Studio Potter,* vol. 1, no. 1, (Fall, 1972), pp. 12–15.

Wulff, Hans E., Wulff, Hildegard S., and Koch, Leo. "Egyptian Faïence, A Possible Survival in Iran," *Archaeology,* vol. no. 2 (April 1968), pp. 98–107.

Wulff, Hans E. *The Traditional Crafts of Persia.* Cambridge, Massachusetts: The MIT Press, 1966.

Manufacturers and Suppliers

Airbrushes

Badger Air-Brush Co.
9128 W. Belmont Avenue
Franklin Park, Illinois 60131

Thayer and Chandler Inc.
215 W. Ohio
Chicago, Illinois 60610

Brushes

Ceramichrome
Box A
Stanford, Kentucky 40484

L. Reusche and Co.
2–6 Lister Ave.
Newark, New Jersey 07105

Ceramic Fiber Blanket

Cerafiber
Johns-Manville
1601 23rd St.
Denver, Colorado 80216

Fiberfrax®
Carborundum Company
Insulation Division
Box 808
Niagara Falls, New York 14302

Insblanket
A. P. Green Refractory Co.
Mexico, Missouri 65265

Ceramic Silkscreen Colors

American Art Clay Co. (AMACO)
4717 W. Sixteenth St.
Indianapolis, Indiana 46222

China Paint

Powdered
L. Reusche and Co.
2–6 Lister Ave.
Newark, New Jersey 07105

Semimoist
American Art Clay Co. (AMACO)
4717 W. Sixteenth St.
Indianapolis, Indiana 46222

Premixed
CeramiCorner
Box 516
Azusa, California 91702

Philadelphia Ceramics
6017 Keystone St.
Philadelphia, Pennsylvania 19135

CINVA-Ram Block Press

(U.S. Importer)
Schrader Bellows
200 W. Exchange St.
Akron, Ohio 44309

Decals

Ready Made
CeramiCorner
Box 516
Azusa, California 91702

Philadelphia Ceramics
6017 Keystone St.
Philadelphia, Pennsylvania 19135

Custom Made
Art Decal Co.
1145 Loma Ave.
Long Beach, California 90804
(minimum order – 125)

Graphic Art Service
Box 584
Monrovia, California 91016
(minimum order – 125)

Photo Decals
International Decal Corp.
3332 Commercial Ave.
Northbrook, Illinois 60062
(no minimum order)

Underglaze Decals
Commercial Decal Inc.
Specialty Division
Box 747
East Liverpool, Ohio 43920
(minimum order – 500)

Decal Medium and Pigment

L. Reusche and Co.
2–6 Lister Ave.
Newark, New Jersey 07105

Decal Paper

Advance Process Supply Co.
400 N. Noble St.
Chicago, Illinois 60622

General Ceramic Supplies

American Art Clay Co. (AMACO)
4717 W. Sixteenth St.
Indianapolis, Indiana 46222

Diamond Ceramics
255 Worcester Rd.
Westboro, Massachusetts 01581

Eagle Ceramics Inc.
12266 Wilkins Ave.
Rockville, Maryland 20852

Glaze, Stain, Underglaze

Ceramichrome
Box A
Stanford, Kentucky 40484

Drakenfeld Colors
Hercules Incorporated
Box 519
Washington, Pennsylvania 15301

Duncan Ceramic Products
Box 7827
Fresno, California 93727

Mayco
20800 Dearborn St.
Chatsworth, California 91311

Luster Glaze

Hanovia Hobby Products
1 W. Central Ave.
East Newark, New Jersey 07029

Med-Mar Metals
Box 6453
Anaheim, California 92806

L. Reusche and Co.
2–6 Lister Ave.
Newark, New Jersey 07105

Molds

Ceramichrome
Box A
Stanford, Kentucky 40484

Duncan Ceramic Products
Box 7827
Fresno, California 93727

Photoclay Kits

Picceramic
817 Ethel Place
Vestal, New York 13850

Raku Kilns

Peach Valley Pottery
311 West 7th
Carthage, Missouri 64836

Silkscreen Materials

Advance Process Supply Co.
400 N. Noble St.
Chicago, Illinois 60622

Temperature Equivalents for Orton Standard Pyrometric Cones

Cone Number	Large Cones		Small Cones	
	¹ 60°C	108°F	300°C	540°F
022	585°C	1085°F	630°C	1165°F
021	602	1116	643	1189
020	625	1157	666	1231
019	668	1234	723	1333
018	696	1285	752	1386
017	727	1341	784	1443
016	764	1407	825	1517
015	790	1454	843	1549
014	834	1533	870	1596
013	869	1596	880	1615
012	876	1609	900	1650
011	886	1627	915	1680
†010	887	1629	919	1686
09	915	1679	955	1751
08	945	1733	983	1801
07	973	1783	1008	1846
06	991	1816	1023	1873
05	1031	1888	1062	1944
04	1050	1922	1098	2008
03	1086	1987	1131	2068
02	1101	2014	1148	2098
01	1117	2043	1178	2152
1	1136	2077	1179	2154
2	1142	2088	1185	2165
3	1152	2106	1196	2185
4	1168	2134	1209	2208
5	1177	2151	1221	2230
6	1201	2194	1255	2291
7	1215	2219	1264	2307
8	1236	2257	1300	2372
9	1260	2300	1317	2403
10	1285	2345	1330	2426

† Iron-free (white) are made in numbers 010 to 3. The iron-free cones have the same deformation temperatures as the red equivalents when fired at a rate of 60 Centigrade degrees per hour in air.

Notes:

1. The temperature equivalents in this table apply only to Orton Standard Pyrometric Cones, *when heated at the rates indicated, in an air atmosphere.*

2. Temperature Equivalents are given in degrees Centigrade (°C) and the corresponding degrees Fahrenheit (°F). The rates of heating shown at the head of each column of temperature equivalents were maintained during the last several hundred degrees of temperature rise.

3. The temperature equivalents were determined at the National Bureau of Standards by H. P. Beerman (see Journal of the American Ceramic Society, Vol. 39, 1956).

4. The temperature equivalents are not necessarily those at which cones will deform under firing conditions different from those under which the calibrating determinations were made. For more detailed technical data, please write the Orton Foundation.

5. Conversion Factors: *Centigrade to Fahrenheit* N × 9 ÷ 5 + 32; *Fahrenheit to Centigrade* N − 32 × 5 ÷ 9.

   Courtesy: The Edward Orton Jr. Ceramic Foundation, 1445 Summit Street, Columbus, Ohio 43201

Index

Index to Photographs of Work by Contemporary Artists

About the Author

Leon I. Nigrosh studied architecture at Carnegie Institute of Technology, received his BFA in ceramics from Rhode Island School of Design, and his MFA from Rochester Institute of Technology. Upon graduation, he became the studio manager of the Greenwich House Pottery School in New York. He has been head of the ceramic department at the Craft Center, Worcester, Massachusetts, and a visiting professor at Rhode Island College. In addition to teaching and lecturing, Mr. Nigrosh continues to work in clay. He has had many one-artist shows and his work has been exhibited throughout the country. He has also executed a number of architectural commissions. His writing has appeared in *Craft Horizons* and *School Arts*. He is the author of *Claywork: Form and Idea in Ceramic Design*.